Music of the First Nations

Music in American Life

A list of books in the series appears at the end of this book.

Music of the First Nations

Tradition and Innovation in Native North America

Edited by
TARA BROWNER

UNIVERSITY OF ILLINOIS PRESS
Urbana and Chicago

Library of Congress Cataloging-in-Publication Data
Music of the first nations : tradition and innovation in
native North America / edited by Tara Browner.
    p.   c.m. — (Music in American life)
Includes bibliographical references and index.
ISBN 978-0-252-02221-0 (cloth : alk. paper)
1. Indians of North America—Music—History and criticism.
2. Ethnomusicology—United States—History.
3. Indian dance—North America.
I. Browner, Tara
ML3557.M87   2008
781.62'97—dc22   2008032923

Contents

Acknowledgments

I could not have completed this volume without the help and encouragement of friends, colleagues, and most of all the many patient authors, some of whom waited more than ten years for it to come to press. As with countless essay collections, this one was pieced together a bit at a time over almost a decade. It was a complex project, needing balance among different cultural areas, research methodologies, and historical eras. Meeting those requirements was the primary reason that assembling the collection took as long as it did. Nevertheless, I am grateful to those authors who stayed the course and did not withdraw their submissions for publication in other venues.

Special thanks goes to Ben Harbert, who so beautifully reconfigured the musical examples into a format that would work for publication in a book with specific size limitations. I also appreciate the thorough readings given by my referees, and the work and support of Judith McCulloh and Laurie Matheson at the University of Illinois Press. Finally, I would like to express my appreciation to the UCLA Institute of American Cultures, whose funding was crucial to completing this volume.

Music of the First Nations

Introduction
Studying First Nations
and Inuit Music

TARA BROWNER

In countless ways, the study of North American indigenous musical cultures by Westerners has been a crucial element in establishing ethnomusicology as a discipline distinct from historical musicology. Early ethnologists such as Alice Fletcher, Francis Densmore, James Mooney, and Jesse Walker Fewkes laid the foundations for studying music in its cultural context, with Fewkes making the first known field recordings in 1889. Theodore Baker's *Über die Musik der nordamerikanischen Wilden* (On the Music of the North American Savages), written in 1881 for the University of Leipzig and published in 1882, is probably the first dissertation on an ethnomusicological topic. And Franz Boas included music in his discussion of Northwest Coast culture, with his student George Herzog playing a pivotal role in the founding of an American branch of ethnographic music research. Although most often viewed through the lens of contemporary theoretical models as dated and perhaps even suspect, this body of research stressed the concept of fieldwork as the primary research method, a principle still central in the work of ethnomusicologists.

In recent years, however, the amount of research done on First Nation music has decreased somewhat, especially south of the U.S.–Canadian border. There are any number of reasons, ranging from research funding issues (it is often easier to get research funding for projects outside of the United States) to working out just how music might fit into the new emphasis on applied indigenous studies seen in many American Indian studies programs. But undoubtedly the most difficult challenge to research is the antipathy of Indians themselves, who have become less than enthusiastic about being "studied" since the mid-1970s. In the time of Densmore, ethnologists could simply show up, and with the reservation agent applying appropriate pressures (or in the case of Densmore a sibling using her charms), recordings could be made, photographs taken, and people's lives turned into ethnographic description. By contemporary standards, recording technology was the most problematic ethnographic device, and it was common for recordings and transcriptions made during this era to be copyrighted by the Bureau of American Ethnology, as if by recording the songs ethnologists and their funding agencies *owned* them. But the combination of the civil rights movement (and in Indian country the American Indian Movement) and an increasing awareness of tribal sovereignty changed all that, and many Indians and tribal governments are increasingly wary of "anthros" of any stripe.

Today's scholars of Native music are the direct intellectual descendants of Densmore and Fletcher, but with some telling differences in methodology, field methods, and outlook. First, contemporary research is much more community based and oriented, with service to Native peoples as a primary goal; second, human subjects concerns and intellectual property issues have come to the disciplinary forefront, making it virtually impossible to simply appear on a reservation or reserve and start recording; and third, Indian people themselves are much more involved in the directions that research is evolving in their communities. It was in this spirit that this volume was conceptualized, with the goals of Native participation in the project and usefulness to multiple constituencies (mainstream academic through tribal college) central to the process of soliciting and assembling the text.

Each essay in this anthology presents a specific issue or set of issues significant to the Native people whose music is being discussed and reflects the diversity of approaches to Native North American music, from non-Native academic scholarship to the experiences of a traditional Native performer of tribal songs. In the interest of providing a balance between the views of cultural insiders and outsiders, a significant number of authors are Native, and one essay has been cowritten by Native and non-Native scholars. The text is ordered so that tribal-specific music is presented first (see Figure I.1 for the geographic locations of the tribal peoples discussed), whereas the last two essays discuss the Pan-Indian topics of pow-wows and country music. But perhaps the most important facet of the collection is how it illustrates *the many ways of doing contemporary ethnomusicology in Indian country,* from dialogic (von Rosen), coauthored with a Native specialist (Lafferty and Keillor), primarily historiographic (Vander), and fieldwork based (Conlon, Aplin) to using intensive formalistic musical analysis (Draper), linguistic analysis (Sercombe), and interpretive (Browner, Samuels).

In the first essay, "Iglulik Inuit Drum-Dance Songs," Paula Conlon discusses how Inuit songs provide a way to maintain links with the past through a traditional musical style that dominates not only the Iglulik but also the larger Inuit population from the Arctic East to West: the drum-dance song. In the Iglulik region the man composes the drum-dance song and teaches it to his wife, who in turn teaches it to the other women in the community for public performance in the *qaggi*, the large ceremonial igloo. At the drum dance, the women sing while the composer dances and plays a single-frame drum, with the drum being hit with a wooden mallet on the frame and *not* on the skin. This study endeavors to provide a glimpse into Inuit culture through a discussion of the drum-dance songs that so aptly reflect the lives of the people.

Lucy Lafferty and Elaine Keillor's "Musical Expressions of the Dene: Dogrib Love and Land Songs" describes how the Dene/Dogrib usage of traditional music and dance has been a means by which the Dene have managed to maintain their distinctiveness and culture in their homeland, "Denedeh." Dene Love Songs, which can be sung by men or women, are concerned with personal relationships, and their texts are frequently humorous. Another type of Dene/Dogrib "Love Song" is used to express "love of the land." This essay concentrates on Dogrib musical expressions in these forms, how they relate to the worldview of the Dene people, and how they compare to and differ from other traditional musical expressions of the Dene.

In "The Story of Dirty Face: Power and Song in Western Washington Coast Salish Myth Narratives," Laurel Sercombe illustrates the role of music in the oral literature of the Pacific Northwest Coast region. Often these stories have short songs embedded within the text, by which the various characters speak and sing directly through the storyteller to the audience in a dramatic rendering of the mythological past. Sercombe, who has been involved in various Lushootseed language projects with Coast Salish elder Vi Hilbert for more than a decade, uses her essay to draw critical attention to the essential place of song and language within this dramatic context.

Franziska von Rosen chose to use a dialogic method in her work with singer Margaret Paul in "Drum, Songs, Vibrations: Conversations with a Passamaquoddy Traditional Singer." The focus of this essay and interview is the current Maliseet/Passamaquoddy musical revitalization as experienced and articulated by Paul, who with a small group of traditionalists from St. Mary's reserve has been at the heart of this revival—

bringing back the drum, the songs, the ceremonies, and the way of life that are respectful of these traditions. This discussion centers on those issues that Paul views as vital to an understanding of the music.

"Identity, Retention, and Survival: Contexts for the Performance of Native Choctaw Music" is the result of David E. Draper's work with traditional Choctaw communities in Mississippi during the 1970s and '80s. Illustrated with dense musical transcriptions, Draper's thesis centers on his concept of the "occasion" in Choctaw music, in which musical performances are inexorably linked with specific community events. According to Draper, without the event, or occasion, to spur performance of specific musical repertories, the music no longer has meaning within its community context, and its performance often ceases. Draper's theoretical linkage between music and event is comparable to the anthropological theory of concomitant variation.

In "This Is Our Dance": The Fire Dance of the Fort Sill Chiricahua Warm Springs Apache," T. Christopher Aplin discusses the role of music in retaining identity in the diasporic Apache community of Fort Sill, Oklahoma. Descendants of the Chiricahua Apache who were exiled from Arizona to Oklahoma following the defeat of Geronimo in 1886, the Fort Sill Apache struggle with language loss and maintaining themselves as Tiné People in a sea of southern Plains tribes such as the Kiowa and Comanche, whose pow-wow and Gourd Dance cultures threaten to erode the distinctiveness of Chiricahua ceremonialism and musical expression.

Judith Vander, in "The Creative Power and Style of Ghost Dance Songs," gives a very brief description of the Ghost Dance religion, and then focuses on two main points. First, Ghost Dance performance rests on an underlying premise: a belief that dance, music, and poetic song texts have the power to affect the spiritual world. Second, she emphasizes that the simple-complex style of Ghost Dance music and poetic song texts is a remarkable artistic achievement.

My own essay, "An Acoustic Geography of Intertribal Pow-wow Songs," concerns the broad binary of Northern-Southern by which scholars (and Indians) tend to group pow-wow musical styles. I argue that somewhere between Northern-Southern and tribal-specific singing there are smaller regional modes of vocal performance that can be discerned by a deep listening for musical elements such as vocal timbre, range, and ornamentation usually overlooked in ethnographic accounts of music, and that all too often the songs themselves are lost within the ethnographic details.

Finally, in "Singing Indian Country," David Samuels writes about the processes by which Anglo-American country western music has been

"Indianized," to the point where it sonically represents Indians as well. Samuels asks, "How can the sounds of white, hardscrabble, blue-collar, evangelical Christian, sometimes racist ideologies be embraced by the very people against whom those ideologies have often been so destructively employed?" Problematizing the old theoretical warhorse of "acculturation," Samuels foregrounds the notion of Indian agency in the choice of what musical genres of the dominant society are to be embraced and recontextualized to represent the Native experience.

In conclusion, I would like to note that David Draper's essay was first published in 1980 under the title "Occasions for the Performance of Native Choctaw Music" in the UCLA Department of Ethnomusicology's *Selected Reports in Ethnomusicology 3*. This newly titled version is a significant revision of that essay, which I felt deserved a broader audience. All other contributions were written specifically for this anthology.

Figure I.1. Map of North America. Courtesy of Tara Browner.

1

Iglulik Inuit
Drum-Dance Songs

PAULA CONLON

This article discusses the traditional musical style that dominates the Inuit from the Arctic East to West: the drum-dance song, or *pisiq* (plural *pisiit*).[1] The syllabic *a-ya-ya*, which appears in the text of drum-dance songs from Alaska to Greenland, is used today to designate the whole of the song as well. The 315 drum-dance songs that provide the basis for this study are from the Iglulik Inuit area of northern Baffin Island. The songs were collected from the following hamlets: Mittimatalik (Pond Inlet) (collected by Jean-Jacques Nattiez in 1976 and 1977), Igloolik (Nattiez in 1977), and Ikpiarjuk (Arctic Bay) (Lorne Smith in 1964 and Paula Conlon in 1985) (see figure 1.1).[2]

The Iglulik Inuit of the present day are descended from the people who brought the Thule culture into the Baffin Island area around AD 1200. In 1822 Captains William Edward Parry and George Francis Lyon of the Royal Navy spent the winter at Igloolik during their search for the Northwest Passage from the Atlantic to the Pacific oceans. When ethnologists Knud Rasmussen, Peter Freuchen, and Therkel Matthiassen arrived in Igloolik in 1921, they found the way of life still very much as it had been one hundred years before. Hunting was the chief activity, with char fishing as a supplementary activity performed by women (NWT 1990–91: 168).

The period 1920–60 has been referred to as the era of the "big three": the Royal Canadian Mounted Police, the Hudson's Bay Company, and the missions (Mary-Rousselière 1984: 443). In the 1960s, the Canadian gov-

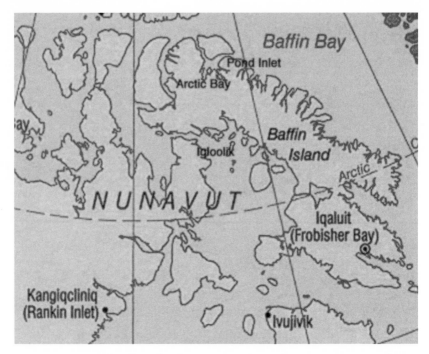

Figure 1.1. Map of Baffin Island. Courtesy of Tara Browner. Map template taken from public domain collection of the Perry-Castañeda Map Collection, University of Texas at Austin.

ernment began systematically regrouping the Inuit around these installations. Modern aluminum houses were built in the hamlets of Admiralty Inlet, Sanirajak (Hall Beach), Igloolik, Ikpiarjuk, and Mittimatalik, and the government set up federal schools in Igloolik (1959), Mittimatalik (1960), and Ikpiarjuk (1962), with compulsory education for all children ages six to sixteen. The Inuit move freely among these communities, but the nomadic way of life, based on hunting and fishing, disappeared in fewer than ten years.

As the fieldwork for this study was carried out after the government's regrouping of the Inuit in the 1960s, these songs were all collected "artificially." The singers were asked to sing for the sole purpose of being recorded, with the result that the musical style of the recordings was sometimes affected by contact with white musical civilization and modern conditions of performance. In this sense, the collection represents the musical state of the Iglulik Inuit between 1964 and 1985 (Conlon 1992).[3]

Song Composition

Traditionally, a man composed a drum-dance song in solitude, usually while hunting. Once he had decided on the text and the melody, he repeated the song over and over so as not to forget it. When the hunter returned home, he taught the song to his wife, who in turn taught it to the other women in the village, to be ready for a public performance at the feasts *(qarginiq)*. The women's role is paramount because "the woman is supposed to be the man's memory" (Rasmussen 1929: 240). When the composer was a visitor, he taught his song to the women of the host camp before the drum dance (Uyarak 1977).

There is no report, either from ethnographic sources or from consultants, of women *dancing* with the drum in the Iglulik area.[4] Rasmussen notes that every man and woman, and some of the children, may have their own songs (with appropriate melodies) that can be sung in the *qaggi* (dance house) (1929: 227), but there is no information about how the women's songs are presented. Of the 147 drum-dance songs (of known authorship) from Igloolik, Ikpiarjuk, and Mittimatalik, only 4 are attributed to female composers.

Although the character of Iglulik Inuit drum-dance songs is *personal,* this is not in the sense of property such as that exhibited by some North American Indian cultures. For instance, it is not necessary to ask permission before singing someone else's song (Nattiez 1988: 45). An indication of the lack of possessiveness of songs is the availability of portions of common text in personal songs by different composers. During my fieldwork in Ikpiarjuk in 1985, many of the singers spoke about the communal aspect of the singing of another's songs, saying that public acknowledgment of the original creator of the song was sufficient. Interviews from Nattiez's fieldwork in 1976 and 1977 indicate a similar attitude toward song ownership at Mittimatalik and Igloolik.

Song Texts

The text in drum-dance songs is in large part linked to basic experiences in the Inuit way of life. Topics of songs include hunting, people, death, *qallunaaq* (white man), singing, and religion. As hunting is essential for survival and is the primary activity during which songs are created, it is not surprising to find that the theme of 68.5 percent of the song texts revolves around some aspect of hunting, as in this song: "The polar bear over there, I see it over there, ayaya . . . My harpoon, I suddenly want it now, ayaya. . . . My dogs there, I suddenly want them now, ayaya . . ." (Panipakoochoo 1977: 5d-84.PI77-10).[5]

The *qallunaaq* category (4 percent of songs) includes eight versions of a song dealing with "this little hook," a feature of the syllabic alphabet used by missionaries in biblical translations (*NWT* 1990–91: 196). Whalers brought examples of these syllabic-print Bibles to Mittimatalik before the arrival of the missionaries in 1922 (Qango 1977), but the Inuit had no instruction in the use of the alphabet. The text is: "This little hook shape, I wish I could find out what it is, ayaya, I-E-OO-A-pie-pee-poo-pa, ayaya" (L. Kalluk 1985: 4g-3.AB85-30).

Songs listed under "singing" (4 percent of songs) deal with the process of composition and the frustration of attempting to create something new: "It turns out nothing was left for me, no future songs at all, ayaya. . . . Somebody said they were all gone. Our ancestors used up all the songs, ayaya . . ." (Ikaliiyuk 1977: 5e-15.IGL77-88).

Drum Construction

The Inuit drum *(qilaut)* averages approximately seven inches in diameter but is known to vary in diameter from five to thirty-four inches.[6] Drums from the eastern Arctic are typically larger than those found farther west. Figure 1.2 is a drum made by Aglak Atitat of Ikpiarjuk in 1985. Its diameter is twenty-three and a quarter inches.

To construct a drum, a wooden frame is bent by means of steaming and soaking.[7] The frame is then tapered and nailed together in a circle, and the skin is bound tightly to the frame with sinew or string. The same cord that binds the drumhead also ties the drum handle. Like the drum handle, the mallet is roughly shaped to fit the hand. The mallet is then covered with sealskin.

Drum Dances

Traditional drum dances were part of song festivals that usually took place in a large igloo called a *qaggi*, which could hold up to one hundred people. In order to announce a drum dance, someone would go out and shout for everybody to come over: "It was just like a community hall" (Uyarak 1977). In the *qaggi*, drum-dance competitions took place that generally involved the whole community. These festivals occurred when there was abundant food and generally started with a communal feast of caribou and seal. Festivals took place principally in autumn or winter, and sometimes took place between teams from different camps. Isapee Qango (from Igloolik) said that the length of the feast was usually around three days but could last up to five days (1977). Rasmussen notes that when there were visitors, the entertainment might go on all

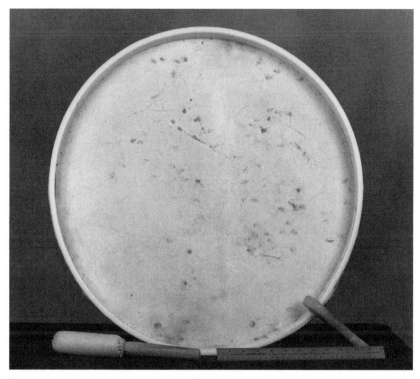

Figure 1.2. Iglulik Inuit drum (maker: Aglak Atitat; collector: Paula Conlon; acquisition date: 1985).

night, throughout the dark hours, which could be up to all twenty-four (1929: 228, 230).

No matter what form the competition took, there was clearly a winner. Along with the prestige gained, tangible prizes (such as harpoons) were sometimes awarded. The success of the song festival depended on the daily practicing of the songs by each family (Rasmussen 1929: 228). A more contemporary indication of this practice is that by François Quassa of Igloolik: "His mother-in-law used to sing a lot. . . . They used to live in one igloo, the whole family, in-laws, and everything. And she used to sing every night, before they went to sleep" (1977).

Structure of the Drum Dance

At the beginning of the festival, the drum *(qilaut)* was placed on the ground in the center of the *qaggi.* Any composer could start. When he took the drum, his wife began to sing his song. His wife was the leader *(ingirtuq)* of the choir *(ingiortut)* of women who had learned the song. The composer *did not sing,* although he cried out from time to time (Urrunaluk 1977).[8] According to Rasmussen, "The *mumirtuq* (the dancer) will . . . often content himself with flinging out a few lines of the text, while his wife leads the chorus" (1929: 240). The term *mumerneq,* which means "changing about," signifies the combination of the melody, the words, and the dance (Rasmussen 1929: 228).

While drum dancing, the man dances slightly bent over, holding the drum with his left hand (a left-handed man holds the drum in the right hand). With his wrist he pivots the drum from right to left. He uses the mallet *(katutarq),* covered with sealskin, to hit the wooden frame, alternately on the base *(akkirtarpuq)* and the top *(anaulirpuq)* of the drum. The feet are often synchronized with the beat of the drum to avoid fatigue (Urrunaluk 1977). Some drummers are so skillful in the handling of the drum that they can make it pivot in the air from side to side without holding the handle (Iyetuk 1977; Kupak 1977).

When the first dancer at a drum dance was finished, another took his place. The elder men present evaluated the merits of each song and dance. Although the competitive character of the traditional drum dance could take various forms, it was mainly a test of endurance to determine the capacity of the dancer to "hold the beat." The longer the song, the heavier the drum seemed to become, and the large size of the drums from the eastern Arctic contributed to the difficulty. The number of songs known was also taken into consideration. In the hamlet of Igloolik, the song was said to wrap itself inside the wooden frame of the drum (Iyetuk 1977; Urrunaluk 1977), and the drum itself was considered responsible for the hardship of performing (Ikaliiyuk 1977).

Song Cousins and Song Duels

The competition could involve all the men participating at a festival, but often it was specifically between *illuqiik* (singular *illuq*), that is, "song cousins." This strong friendship was formed by mutual consent, signified by an exchange of wives, pleasantries, and food. At the feasts, song cousins took turns confronting each other with insult songs *(iviut).* But as Rasmussen points out, "Song cousins may very well expose each other in their respective songs, and thus deliver home truths, but it must always be done in a humorous form, and in words so chosen as to excite no feeling among the audience but that of merriment" (1929: 23).

Drum-dance competitions were also used to resolve serious disputes and involved vicious songs of derision. Rasmussen describes the song duel: "Here, no mercy must be shown; it is indeed considered manly to expose another's weakness with the utmost sharpness and severity; but behind all such castigation there must be a touch of humour, for mere abuse in itself is barren, and cannot bring about any reconciliation" (1929: 231).

Social humiliation was the principal means of defeating one's opponent, although these tournaments could be accompanied by physical confrontation as well (for example, boxing). Once the song duel was finished, the social equilibrium was restored. The quarrel became a thing of the past, and presents were exchanged to show that friendship had been reestablished (Rasmussen 1929: 232).

The song duel had a judicial character to resolve disputes peacefully, involving the entire community as the "jury," but the drum dance also provided a social diversion, especially welcome during the long, dark winter months. Therefore, the drum dance and the drum-dance songs had a multifunctional dimension. They served to draw the people together and eased tensions arising from daily living in a close-knit community.

The Drum Dance Today

The drum-dance songs of this study were only rarely performed in the field situation with a drum (only 41 of 315 songs collected between 1964 and 1985). I was told that drum dances used to be held in the community center at Ikpiarjuk, but they faded in the early 1970s when the hall was closed. The songs with percussion collected from Igloolik and Mittimatalik in 1976 and 1977 were not part of a traditional drum dance, and during my fieldwork at Ikpiarjuk in 1985, I was able to arrange only a "staged" drum dance with two dancers, Aglak Atitat and David Kalluk.

David Kalluk (1985) told me that he and singer Koonoo Ipirq used to "go out to sing" at competitions such as those held at "Toonik Tyme" in nearby Iqaluit (Frobisher Bay). When I contacted government officials in Iqaluit to obtain permission to attend the festival, they warned me that I was not likely to find much traditional music. This proved to be the case, and when I attended Toonik Tyme in Iqaluit in the spring of 1987, the only drum dancing at the festival consisted of showpieces to open the festivities, performed by Lens Lyberth from East Greenland and Celestin Erkikjuk from Kangiqcliniq (Rankin Inlet).

The Song "I'm So Happy"

I have chosen to discuss the song "I'm So Happy" (5b-2.AB85-4) because of its illustration of the common features of drum-dance songs from the Iglulik area (see musical example 1.1). The title is derived from the first line of the text, a common method of referring to traditional drum-dance songs.

Textual Analysis

Eleven versions of the song "I'm So Happy" were collected from Mittimatalik (1976) and Ikpiarjuk (1985). The omission of this song from the Igloolik corpus suggests that it was known only locally. This song is ascribed to the singer Qargiuq: "One winter, he [Qargiuq] was really sick, with TB, and he thought he was going to die before spring. But he got better again, and when he was hunting seal, in springtime, he sang: 'I'm so glad I'm going to live, to see the spring come again'" (Qango 1977).

The texts show the variations between versions while still retaining the overall meaning. The recurring figure of speech is the appearance of the sunrise, an appropriate moment for the Inuit when the spring arrives after months of darkness. The oxygen mask that appears in versions numbered 5b-9 and 5b-13 (and obliquely in 5b-3: "Let me breathe because I'll be living") refers to the personal experience of the composer, Qargiuq, and his association of his recovery from tuberculosis with spring.

Variations in text show how the story is retained in a number of guises, confirming this set of songs as being concordant. The establishment of an urtext is essential in determining concordances because its different versions can also use a variety of melodies. It is important to keep in mind the Inuit concept of drum-dance songs, as noted by Caribou Inuit Donald Suluk from Arviat (Eskimo Point): "In the Inuit way of listening to songs, you don't really listen to the tune but to what is being said. . . . The song has to be sung completely and followed according to how it's composed. But if it was to be sung, say, with some words missing or with the verses mixed up, it could insult the song's writer or family members" (1983: 28). This emphasis on the story line was indicated again and again to me during my fieldwork when my consultants and interpreters would focus on the text. They would never say, "That is a nice tune."

Form Analysis

As a tone language, Inuktitut, through the text used, influences the melodic contours and pitches used in the songs. This accounts for the number of tone reiterations (unisons) that occur sporadically within a melody. Maija M. Lutz comments on the repetition on the same pitch in certain sections of Inuit songs from Cumberland Peninsula on southern Baffin Island (1978: 57), and this tendency is also noted among the Netsilik Inuit west of Hudson Bay (Cavanagh 1982: 122). Beverley Cavanagh

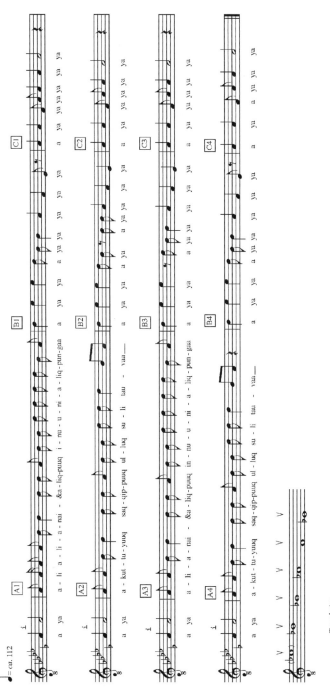

Musical example 1.1. Transcription of Iglulik Inuit drum-dance song "I'm So Happy." Song 5b-2.AB85-4. Transcribed by Paula Conlon.

maintains that rests exist only when a singer needs to take a breath and that the ideal performance would eliminate most breath divisions, creating a continuous melodic line (1982: 95). "The songs are logogenic, or closely derived from speech patterns. . . . Additional syllables are never accommodated by subdividing a beat, but rather by adding another. The words . . . would seem to be the most feasible and the most objective means of identifying 'motives' and examining the structural patterns formed by their combinations. . . . Most, though not all, words are similarly placed when a musical 'motive' reoccurs" (96–97, 133).

For the song "I'm So Happy," I have chosen to divide the melody into three motives based primarily on the word structure. The first part of the melody (motive A on the first line) is sung to translatable text, whereas the second and third motives (motives B and C on the second line) make use of the *ayaya* vocable (syllables without translatable text that nevertheless have "meaning"). The third motive (C) serves to reiterate the tonal center with repeated repetitions on one pitch with the exception of a dip down the interval of a third and back up again at the beginning of the C section. Before each of the A motives is what I have termed an *incipit* (i): portions of the *ayaya* vocable that serve to situate the tonal center. As with the textual analysis, it is important to keep in mind that the melody is subservient to the text; the primary function of the singing is to tell the story and provide a vehicle for the drum dancing.

Drum Rhythm

In the version of the song "I'm So Happy" numbered 5b-14 (recorded in 1976), the singer sings with a metronome marking of the quarter note at a rate of 92 beats per minute, whereas the drummer is performing with a drumbeat at a rate of 100 beats per minute, indicating a significant discrepancy between the tempo of the voice and that of the percussion. The drummer, Joshua Qumangapiq of Mittimatalik, was born in 1905; he was recognized by his peers as being a valuable source of knowledge about the traditional Inuit ways.[9] This version supports the view that the older performers tend to treat the voice and percussion as stratified lines.[10]

In contrast, in the version of "I'm So Happy" numbered 5b-4 (recorded in 1985) the drummer keeps approximately the same beat as the singer (the voice and the drumbeat with the quarter note at a rate of 116 beats per minute), separating only occasionally when the singer's rhythm fluctuates more than the drummer's. The performers of this version are singer Koonoo Ipirq and drummer David Kalluk of Ikpiarjuk, who play together frequently. Kalluk, born in 1945 (two generations later than Qumangapiq), speaks English and has had a lot of contact with white music through the country music that prevails on the radio. The steady pulse of Kalluk's drumming in synch with the singing may be partially accounted for by his exposure to Western music and the familiarity that developed from working closely with Ipirq (born in 1931).

A common performance practice used by the drummer in both versions of the song "I'm So Happy" performed with percussion (that is 5b-14 and 5b-4) is the interjection of periodic yells. In Kalluk's case, he actually says, "Yahoo," a decidedly white influence on an otherwise Inuit text.

Speculations

Ramón Pelinski presents an interesting "test" of an approach to determine if a Westerner can produce a pastiche of an Inuit drum-dance song by following the rules set out by its generative grammar (1981: 157–200). Using the song "I'm So Happy" as a base, one could attempt to "create" a strophic song that uses an octave range, has a pentatonic scale (B♭–G–F–D–C), and creates a three-motive structure made up of a meandering contour (motive A), a descending contour (motive B), and ending with a plateau or relatively flat-line contour (motive C). The plateau contour is sung to the vocable *ayaya* that has tone reiterations on the tonal center (the interval a fourth above the lowest pitch in the song). The singer varies repetitions according to the text, employing numerous tone reiterations on the tonal center, and uses a series of eighth notes with a quarter-note pulse in a moderate tempo. Longer note values occur at the ends of strophes, and subsequent strophes begin with an incipit that repeats the tonal center that prevails in the C motive that precedes the incipit. The text is paramount. Thus, one could create a "pastiche" that can be considered representative of a "typical" drum-dance song from the Iglulik area.

Even, however, to someone with a thorough knowledge of the Inuit language, the texts that determine the musical material of traditional songs are allusive at best, referring to events that were commonly known only at the time of composition, which was why the story behind the song was always requested (although seldom known by my consultants in 1985). One can deduce from the ethnographic literature and an analysis of the corpus of 315 songs what are the preferred musical occasions, type of drum, scales, ranges, forms, tonal centers, melodic contours, tempos, and concordances of Iglulik Inuit drum-dance songs. But one cannot actually know *how* the Inuit composed their songs. Over time there has been a whole repertoire of melodies used in drum-dance songs. The language itself influences the way that a person from a particular culture will shape his or her ideas in sound. According to the Netsilik Inuit poet Orpingalik: "Songs are thoughts, sung out with the breath when people are moved by great forces and ordinary speech no longer suffices" (Rasmussen 1931: 321).

The drum-dance songs are a way for the Inuit to maintain a link with their past. There are also instances of traditional music being used in modern settings. The Anglican priest in Mittimatalik set biblical words to the tune of a drum-dance song, and the song was performed during the Easter ceremonies in 1976. Northern rock bands occasionally use Inuit melodies. On the compact disc *Nitjautiit* (The People's Music), Inuit singer Susan Aglukark performs the song "Old Stories," which combines *ayaya* with boogie-woogie (1991: cut 29).

Although there is no doubt that white culture has made major inroads into the traditional way of life of the Inuit, elements of traditional song still come through. Present-day Inuit composers continue to find ways to express themselves that honor the old ways while selectively utilizing musical influences from the dominant white culture to help get their message across to a contemporary audience. The recontextualization of the *ayaya* repertoire over time has proved to be an effective strategy for preservation, much as their ancestors used traditional drum-dance songs to ensure the transmission of information about the past to future generations.

Notes

1. The native term *Inuit* means "the people." It has replaced the older term *Eskimo* that was formerly used to designate people of the Arctic, an Algonquian Indian term that means "eater of raw meat" that many Inuit people found offensive.

2. When the new territory of Nunavut (Our Land) in the eastern Canadian Arctic was created in 1999, the names of the communities reverted to their original Inuit designations. The hamlets under study are Pond Inlet (Mittimatalik—"the resting place of Mittima"), Arctic Bay (Ikpiarjuk—"the pocket," referring to the mountains surrounding the hamlet by the water), and Igloolik—"a place with igloos" (Missionary Oblates of Mary Immaculate: n.p.).

3. The compact disc *Songs of the Inuit Iglulik: Canada* (2004) includes sixteen drum-dance songs from this corpus.

4. The term *consultant* refers to the Inuit performers of song and dance who agreed to be recorded or interviewed for this project.

5. An explanation of the symbols for song number 5d-84.PI77–10 follows: "5" refers to a five-note scale pattern; "d" is the fourth scale pattern; "84" means that this is the eighty-fourth song using this scale pattern; "PI" refers to Pond Inlet (Mittimatalik), where the song was collected ("AB" indicates Arctic Bay [Ikpiarjuk], and "IGL" indicates Igloolik); "77" is 1977, indicating the year the song was collected; and "10" signifies that this is the tenth song collected on this particular field trip.

6. These drum measurements are from a survey I conducted of twenty-seven

drums from across the Arctic housed at the Canadian Museum of Civilization in Hull, Quebec.

7. Since northern Baffin Island is above the timberline, in precontact times drum frames were made from a curved bone, usually from a whale.

8. In Ikpiarjuk in 1985, the two male drum dancers who performed for me also did not sing, and my consultants reported that this was the norm.

9. Joshua Qumangapiq was respected not only as a drum dancer and bearer of culture in regards to drum-dance songs but also as a shaman (priest) with a large repertoire of sacred songs. When I was collecting songs in Ikpiarjuk in 1985, Levi Kalluk, also a shaman, had the largest repertoire of drum-dance songs, and his songs consistently had the most verses.

10. Drum dancer Aglak Atitat (whose age was "around sixty-five" in 1985) also drummed in a rhythm that was relatively independent of the singer's pace when compared with younger performers. I was told that Atitat frequently passed on knowledge of the old ways to the young people. He regularly gave workshops at the elementary school in Ikpiarjuk about how to make a drum, how to build a kayak, and so on, and he told the old stories to the children. Since Inuit children are taught in their own language, Inuktitut, for the first three years of school, they were able to understand Atitat's stories, whose own childhood predated the establishment of federal schools on Baffin Island with the result that he never learned English.

References

Aglukark, Susan. 1991. *Nitjautiit* [The People's Music]. LP Record CBC-CD3. Compact disc.

Cavanagh, Beverley [Diamond]. 1982. *Music of the Netsilik Eskimo: A Study of Stability and Change.* Vol. 1. Mercury Series no. 82. Ottawa: National Museums of Canada.

Conlon, Paula Thistle. 1992. "Drum-Dance Songs of the Iglulik Inuit in the Northern Baffin Island Area: A Study of Their Structures." Ph.D. diss., University of Montreal.

Ikaliiyuk, Rose. 1977. Personal communication with Jean-Jacques Nattiez in Igloolik.

Iyetuk, Isadore. 1977. Personal communication with Jean-Jacques Nattiez in Igloolik.

Kalluk, David. 1985. Personal communication with Paula Conlon in Ikpiarjuk.

Kalluk, Levi. 1985. Personal communication with Paula Conlon in Ikpiarjuk.

Kupak, Michel. 1977. Personal communication with Jean-Jacques Nattiez in Igloolik.

Lutz, Maija M. 1978. *The Effects of Acculturation on Eskimo Music of Cumberland Peninsula.* Mercury Series no. 41. Ottawa: National Museums of Canada.

Mary-Rousselière, Guy. 1984. "Iglulik." In *Handbook of North American Indians,* edited by David Damas and William Sturtevant, 5:431–46. Washington, D.C.: Smithsonian Institution Press.

Missionary Oblates of Mary Immaculate. n.d. "Nunavut: Canadian Arctic." http://www.arcticomi.ca/index.html.

Nattiez, Jean-Jacques. 1988. "La danse à tambour chez les Inuit igloolik (nord de la Terre de Baffin)." *Recherches Amérindiennes au Québec* 18, no. 4: 37–48.

NWT. 1990–91. *Northwest Territories Data Book, 1990–91.* Yellowknife, Northwest Territories: Outcrop.

Panipakoochoo, Letia. 1977. Personal communication with Jean-Jacques Nattiez in Mittimatalik.

Pelinski, Ramón. 1981. *La musique des Inuit du Caribou: Cinq perspectives méthodologiques.* Montreal: Presses de l'Université de Montréal.

Qango, Isapee. 1977. Personal communication with Jean-Jacques Nattiez in Mittimatalik.

Quassa, François. 1977. Personal communication with Jean-Jacques Nattiez in Igloolik.

Rasmussen, Knud. 1929. "Intellectual Culture of the Iglulik Eskimos." In *Report of the Fifth Thule Expedition, 1921–24.* Vol. 7, paper 1. Copenhagen: Gyldendal-Nordisk.

———. 1931. "The Netsilik Eskimos." In *Report of the Fifth Thule Expedition, 1931.* Vol. 8, papers 1–2. Copenhagen: Gyldendal-Nordisk.

Songs of the Inuit Iglulik: Canada. 2004. Witness World PG 1107. Blue Moon Producciones Discograficas (Barcelona), DL B-47952/04. Compact disc.

Suluk, Donald. 1983. "Some Thoughts on Traditional Inuit Music." *Inuktitut* 54: 24–30.

Urrunaluk, Noah. 1977. Personal communication with Jean-Jacques Nattiez in Igloolik.

Uyarak, Joanasie. 1977. Personal communication with Jean-Jacques Nattiez in Igloolik.

2 Musical Expressions of the Dene

Dogrib Love and Land Songs

LUCY LAFFERTY AND ELAINE KEILLOR

The respected Sahtú Dene elder George Blondin concludes his book of stories by stating, "The important values of Dene—respect for the land and respect for one another—will endure, both here in Denendeh and all over the world" (1990: 246). Those primary values are reinforced within Dene society by means of certain songs that can be called in English "land songs" and "love songs." To understand how these songs reinforce a Dene's personal relationship within the terrain of Denendeh and one's personal relationship within the community, ethnographic and histori- cal documentation of the land, now usually referred to as Denendeh, and traditional personal relationships organized to survive within a harsh climate and a delicate ecosystem will be briefly outlined to place these musical expressions into context.

The Dene of Denendeh

In many of the Athapaskan languages a word similar to *Dene* has meant "people." This term was recognized by Alexander Mackenzie, Sir John Franklin, and Father Emile Petitot whose publications on this area of more than 500,000 square miles appeared during the nineteenth century. Other designations such as "Athapascas" and "Northern Athapascans" (because their languages are related to eight spoken by tribes in Oregon and California as well as a group of seven languages spoken in the South- west, including the Navajo and Apache, referred to as Southern Athapas- cans) have appeared in the literature, but today Dene, or Denesuliné, meaning "people of the barren," refers to the groups recognized as forming the Dene Nation. Its members include the Gwich'in (Kutchin), Dinjii Zhuh (Loucheux), Sahtú-Dene (Bearlake), K'áshot'iné (Hare), Tlichoo (Tichaghe, Dogrib, Alimouspigut, or Attimospiquaies), Dégatheotiné (Gokedé or Slavey), and Denesuliné (Chipewyan or Ikovivinioucks) (*Saskatchewan Indian Cultural Centre Newsletter* 1994a: 13).

The Dene people, also known as Ethénheldéli Dene, meaning "Caribou eaters," live in the Deh-cho (Mackenzie River) drainage system on the tundra, almost all of which is found north of the sixtieth parallel. The area stretches from Lake Athabasca, Alberta, in the South and northward to a point near the Mackenzie Delta, from the Cordilleran region of the Rocky Mountains in the West to the Barren Grounds in the East. Over this vast expanse the boreal forest, consisting largely of jack pine, birch, and spruce, gradually gives way northward to the limits of the timberline. With its massive pink rock outcrops, the landscape features thousands of lakes, including the large Great Bear and Great Slave bodies, as well as many rivers. Although fish grow slowly in these waters, the species of whitefish, trout, pickerel, and pike, among others, abound. Game resources include caribou, moose, wood bison, bear, muskrat, hare, beaver, marten, lynx, mink, and fox. Birds are plentiful, particularly during the migration seasons. Summer, although as brief as three months, provides a rapid growing season with more than twenty hours of daylight for a wide variety of berries such as strawberries, raspberries, saskatoons, rose hips, and other edible plants. The northern part of this area can remain frozen with ice and snow for more than seven months of the year. Consequently, the two dominant seasons are a long winter and short summer separated by brief transitional periods known as "freeze-up" (when the land freezes) and "breakup" (when the ice melts).

Archaeological and linguistic evidence suggests that the Dene are descendants of a culture that thrived in the area more than two thousand years ago. The oral stories of the Dene relate the "explosion of a mountain" and a "flood." Geologists have dated the latest eruption of the White River volcano prior to 525 CE. This may account for a dispersal of peoples over a wide area and the development of different branches of the Northern Athapaskan linguistic family.

The thousand-year-old campsites discovered so far confirm the orally transmitted Dene history through indicating usage by a few families who moved about their immediate terrain, fishing and hunting animals and berries for their needs. In one of his stories, Blondin says, "A long time ago the people lived and camped all over the country, wherever there was food. Sometimes they stayed in large groups, sometimes a few families travelled together, and sometimes one family lived alone" (1990: 20).

With the arrival of non-Dene in this terrain, trade in furs, muskets, rifles, and tea commenced. The Hudson's Bay Company (HBC), the oldest incorporated joint-stock merchandising company in the English-speaking world, was chartered in 1670 with exclusive trading rights in the territory traversed by rivers flowing into Hudson Bay. In 1718 the first Dene group arrived at the HBC post in Churchill (Abel 1993: 54). Gradually, some of the easternmost Dene became middlemen and traders for the HBC, but Dene culture changed only slightly during the 1700s.

By 1788 the North West Company (NWC), a rival trading company with Scots and Métis founders, had organized a new base, Fort Chipewyan on Lake Athabasca, and had organized a system of canoe brigades, provisioned by pemmican from the plains, to bring out up to twenty thousand "made beaver" (prime beaver skin in good condition that was the standard of trade) a year. This infrastructure permitted the Dene's support to Mackenzie for his exploration of the river in 1789. On his trip he observed, "Most eastern bands still moved back and forth from caribou hunting grounds to fisheries, while the western bands continued to congregate at fish lakes, then separated to nearby hunting grounds according to the season and to need" (Abel 1993: 75). Although both the HBC and the NWC were primarily interested in obtaining as many good furs as possible, the Dene were not accustomed to hunting more furs than they needed for their survival, but gradually the goods that could be procured from the forts became ever more desirable. The HBC, unlike the NWC, was dependent on "country" food, that is, provisions brought by the Natives, because importing food was both very expensive and difficult to transport. In his early exploratory attempts around 1770, Samuel Hearne had discovered that it was impossible to survive in the North without the skills of the women. "Women had the skills necessary for manufacturing clothing, snowshoe webbing, moccasins, and nets. They ate little themselves but provided a great deal of food through their own fishing, snaring, and gathering activities" (Abel 1993: 101). The goods that could be obtained at the fort made some of their duties easier. With newly available materials, the women used their sewing skills in adorning articles of clothing with beautiful bead and quillwork. Originally, this work consisted of traditional geometric bands of color, but complex floral designs derived from Métis women and eastern First Nation groups became preeminent.

Unfortunately, the coming of Euro-Canadians into the Dene world brought major hardships in addition to economic and social adjustments. As early as the 1780s an outbreak of smallpox affected many Dene, and there were subsequent major epidemics of measles, whooping cough, dysentery, cholera, and influenza that wiped out hundreds of lives in the years 1819, 1825, 1827, 1835, and 1846. The Dene recognized that these scourges came with the Euro-Canadians, providing yet another reason to avoid going to the forts, if possible. In 1821 the HBC and NWC settled their trade disputes by means of a merger, and by the end of that decade the Edzo-Akaitcho negotiations concluded the retaliatory disputes among the Dene themselves. Although it meant having to catch thousands of fish a year in order to feed them, the Dene began to use teams of dogs like the traders did to transport goods more readily over a long distance. There was frequent controversy over this practice, perhaps because of the Dene belief in the equality of all animal and human creatures as well as the dog origin myth of the Dogribs. In any case, the more frequent visits to forts brought the Dene into contact with Euro-Canadian missionaries who wished to convert these people who in their eyes had no religion.

To survive for thousands of years in Denendeh the people had developed a sophisticated system of individual and community responsibilities guided by esteemed elders who were known for their medicinal and leadership prowess. In the nineteenth century in English these persons were referred to as "prophets."

> As long as the Dene . . . can remember there have been prophets . . . living among them. As children, the prophets, both male and female, were trained by listening to stories of animal people and culture heroes. They were taught to pray, singing the songs of the prophets who had come before them, until they were ready to seek a vision of their own. This early training strengthened their ability to see things that are not apparent to ordinary perception. All the prophets received visions of animal people or animal spirits, visions which could occur either in the bush or in dreams. (Moore and Wheelock 1990: 59)

When missionaries of the Roman Catholic and Protestant faiths began to provide ministrations at the forts for the traders, they brought with them a European worldview that "included different ideas about the status of women, patterns of work and leisure, sexual customs, gambling, and even what constituted acceptable humour. They also provided a very different model of religious leadership" (Abel 1993: 120).

The Dene observed as the main Roman Catholic order the Oblates of Mary Immaculate; the Anglican efforts funded by the Church Missionary Society made their first initiatives in the 1840s. Representatives of both groups took it upon themselves to acquire at least one of the Dene languages and to translate prayers, hymns, catechisms, and biblical passages. Both groups accordingly also began rudimentary schools to teach the Dene how to read. These Christian proselytizers and teachers failed to realize that the Dene had a strong system of values in their own oral tradition.

Dene Values

The *Dene Kede Curriculum Teacher's Resource Manual* prepared by Dene elders describes the learning cycle as never ceasing throughout the life span of the individual. This learning cycle is required for each Dene person to "develop a respectful relationship with the Land, the Spiritual world, other people and (oneself)" (Tatti et al. 1993b: 5). For Dene elders, this learning process is based on input through cultural exposure to Dene values by listening, watching, and questioning. As the person reflects on this input through greater cultural self-awareness, sufficient confidence is gradually attained to produce output in the Dene community by various forms of cultural sharing, such as singing songs, celebrating feasts, and telling stories.

Through this process an individual establishes one's own identity and an awareness of one's surrounding world and culture. That surrounding culture is strongly land based in that a person must know how to relate to, survive on, and cooperate with the characteristics of the terrain in which one is placed. This relationship is closely connected to the other living beings on that terrain, which for the Dene includes animals and plants, as well as people. In amalgamating the information and values concerned with the land, and people, the Dene individual incorporates her or his spirit and self. As is indicated in the bottom portion of figure 2.1, the common denominator for the Dene elders in this process is ever expanding knowledge and usage of "language and art." The singing of personal songs such as love and land songs exemplifies this relationship.

Dene Love and Land Songs

An important part of Dene cultural sharing is the performance of what have been frequently labeled in English "love songs," "love hymns," "country songs," or "personal songs" (*Gowhatso shi ts'et'i* in Dogrib). The Dogrib people use two different labels—*ets'elà* and *ndè gho shi ts'et'i*—for songs referring to love of individuals and love of land. In the Dogrib Dene language a name is provided for something only when it is specifically required for the lifestyle of the culture. For example, a plant will not be given a specific designation in Dogrib Dene unless it is required as a food or for medicinal use. Consequently, these specific names indicate a sense of value for each of these groups of songs. The subsequent observations are based on a total of thirty-three songs, recorded between 1913 and 1995.[1]

The Dogrib *ets'elà* category will be translated in English as "love songs."[2] These unaccompanied songs may express sorrow or longing and might be used while performing some work action. When meaningful text

DENE LEARNING CYCLE

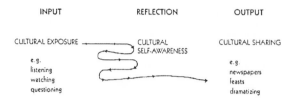

INPUT	REFLECTION	OUTPUT
CULTURAL EXPOSURE	CULTURAL SELF-AWARENESS	CULTURAL SHARING
e.g. listening watching questioning		e.g. newspapers feasts dramatizing

DENE SUBJECT INTEGRATION

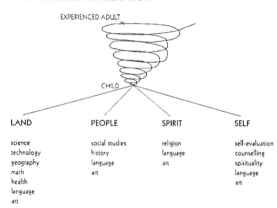

EXPERIENCED ADULT

CHILD

LAND	PEOPLE	SPIRIT	SELF
science	social studies	religion	self-evaluation
technology	history	language	counselling
geography	language	art	spirituality
math	art		language
health			art
language			
art			

Figure 2.1. Top: Dene learning cycle. Courtesy of Lucy Lafferty. Bottom: Dene subject integration. Courtesy of Lucy Lafferty and Dene Kene Education (GNWT–Department of Education).

is present, it can frequently be of a humorous or teasing nature. A song is tied to the specific time when the informant first received or heard the song, and thus each one can recall a historical event or personal incident. In fact, younger generations cannot visualize what is being sung when they do not know the background or event of the song.

Informant Alexis Mackenzie sang one that was used by a woman, Ts'ekots'ìa, to her husband with the text "Old man, old man." It then proceeds with untranslatable words to tease him about his age. Often there is a play on words that seems to be fabricated or inserted between vocables while the person of the opposite sex is addressed as "sister" or "brother." One female informant stated, "It is only when we are young ladies, when we reach a certain age [that] we sing to the one we love. . . . Those songs are not sung to strangers or in an artificial setting."

Accordingly, it seems there are two subcategories for Dogrib Dene *ets'elà*. One type is used publicly as a teasing song to make people laugh and perhaps as a kind of "in-joke" when a particular person may be inferred as the object of the song. The other subcategory would contain what has been termed in Euro-American culture "happy love songs" (Rogers 1989: 94), but for the Dene these songs are very private.

For both subcategories it seems that the texts are largely constructed by the performers and often made up on the spot. Among the recorded "love songs" used for this study, few texts could be completely deciphered and then translated into English. Of course, because Dogrib has only recently been put into a written form of language, there are several dialects spoken, each specific to a particular area. Consequently, even a skilled Dogrib speaker will not recognize the complete vocabulary of all of these dialects. Some of the texts deliberately indicate how the singer is playing with sound to invent his or her text. An example of this practice is the song of informant William Tinqui, translated into English as follows:

> I was with my girlfriend for a while
> Then the plane took me away
> It sounds just like this dooorrrooo
>
> Stay one more night
> She told me, stay one more night
> The plane took me away
> It sounds just like this dooorrrooo.

Ndè gho shi ts'et'i can be literally translated in English as "land for song we have," but are usually referred to as love-of-the-land songs, or occasionally country songs. These songs are closely tied to the land of Denendeh and the area in which the singer was born or experienced significant events in his or her life. For example, Elizabeth Chocolate performed one in which she usually sang "while cutting up meat in the barren land." Its translatable text is as follows:

> It is very beautiful in the barren land.
> Here I am _____.
> As long as we live we may not have another chance _____.
> It sounds very beautiful.

For the Dene Dogrib these two song genres, the love songs and the love-of-the-land songs, are sharply distinguished by the textual content and the performance context. Obviously, the first genre in its publicly presented subcategory is directed to a group of people, even if only a single person is indicated by the text. The subcategory of this genre consists of songs directed to a single person in private situations. Similarly, the love-of-the-land songs are often used in private situations, but it is acceptable for other individuals to overhear these outbursts of praise for the physical surroundings. In some cases the texts for the latter seem to indicate that others should hear the songs as a means of passing on information. For example, a love-of-the-land song performed by Marie Adele Rabesca indicates where caribou, the basic resource for the Dene, are to be found at the end of Lac La Martre.

Musically, many of the examples are organized structurally with two different musical phrases, each of which can be varied in repetition. It appears that these musical gestures are ones that have been passed on for generations within this culture, although individual performers can modify the gesture to their own textural needs. The basis for this argument is that two contemporary occurrences of an opening musical gesture can be found in a song that J. Alden Mason has labeled a "love song" recorded in 1913. That gesture occurs at the beginning of Elizabeth Chocolate's song. Furthermore, it may be that at least in certain parts of Denendeh a particular gesture or a variant thereof is usually connected with love-of-the-land songs. One informant provided three different ones. Although rhythmically the tunes differ and the text determines the repetition of pitches and usually duration, all three songs use gestures that are similar in melodic contour.

The opening gesture of a wide leap upward followed by a slight descent does not occur in the love songs examined. Instead, their gestures tend to have intervals of a more narrow range, often beginning at the highest point and gradually working their way down to the lowest pitch. That low pitch is often separated from the other pitches of the phrase by a break or taking of a breath, as illustrated in figure 2.2. This characteristic is typical of other genres of traditional Dene songs.

These melodic-contour distinctions also do not seem to be based on gender, as each of these profiles can be found in the repertoire of both men or women. The only gender difference may be that men appear more willing to perform the teasing, humorous love songs than women. Because traditionally in Dene society marriages were arranged through the consent of parents and elders so that a woman belonged to her parents until released by her father to another man, the culture may have frowned on women even singing about their own desires in love songs (Ryan 1995: 49).

The timbral vocal quality used for these unaccompanied songs, both love songs and songs of the land, appears to be similar in a spectral analysis of female and male performers. As illustrations using a computer-based analytic system (McGee and Merkley 1991) indicate, the emphasis on the first upper partial is quite similar for both performances given.

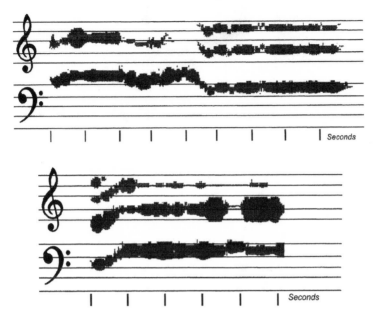

Figure 2.2. *Ndè gho shi ts'et'i.* Top: Spectral analysis of example sung by Morris Mendo. The structure of the whole song is A B, then five times C D. The analytic portion of one of the variants of the D phrase shows the change of vocal production and the extension of the resting tone at the end of the phrase. Bottom: Spectral analysis of example sung by Adeline Vital. The structure of the whole song is seven times the A phrase, seven times the B phrase, three times the C phrase, plus a new lower variant of A three times. The analytic portion is of one of the C phrases showing the generally strong harmonic stricture of the octave and fifth and the long, sustained, pulsating use of the resting tone at the end.

Comparisons with Other Traditional Dene Songs

Although in the past there were probably a wider range of songs than used today in the culture, the Dene still have a large number of traditional songs used with dances and for hand games (Helm and Lurie 1966). An evening of traditional dance is referred to as *Toghà Dagowo* in Dogrib, meaning "all night dance," and is often translated in English as Tea Dance.

During the past two decades such an event opens with at least one prayer song *(Nàdats'e ti zhi)* during which the group of male singers uses a gentle tap on at least one of the available handheld single-headed drums while everyone else stands still, facing inward in a circle, looking down reverentially.[3] Structurally, these songs often use two main phrases in various permutations such as ABB'ABB' or ABA'B. The resultant con-tour is normally one that leaps up to a higher point at the opening or begins approximately the interval of a fifth above the final resting tone and gradually descends through both gestures (Keillor 1986: 68; Beaudry 1992: 84). The vocal production preferred for the performance of prayer songs is one with a quavering, nasal quality. None of the renditions of love and land songs in the recorded collection uses the pulsating vocal quality that provides the particular timbral character of the songs used for the *Toghà Dagowo.* The songs actually accompanying dancing have a more pronounced use of this quality, as the men must project their voices above strong drumbeats being used in the Drum Dance songs *(Eye t'a dagowo)* whether for the clockwise circle formation, the Couple's Dance *(Do nàke lìła yagito t'a dagowo),* or the Line Dance *(Nàkea k'e dagowo)* (Keillor 1986, Beaudry 1992).[4]

Although the performance of the songs connected with traditional social dancing never completely disappeared from Dene culture, there has been during the past two decades a concerted effort by the Dene leaders to emphasize the importance of their musical traditions through educational and other means. That is why recordings of elders singing love songs and love-of-the-land songs are now regularly incorporated into the school curriculum. To return to the Dene charts of how an individual learns and then gives back to one's society, there is an emphasis on art and culture in all four divisions of LAND PEOPLE SPIRIT SELF.

According to the Dene elders, listening to and learning songs of the land can inculcate enjoyment of the land, increase self-confidence in managing the land, provide understanding of the importance of the land for survival and how all of its creatures are interrelated, engender appre-ciation for how the Dene obtain food from the land with their technology, furnish knowledge of the importance of being familiar with the land as specific locations, develop skills to be able to survive on the land, and be familiar with the traditional ways of being on the land (Tatti et al. 1993a: xxxvi). All of these values are closely tied to the absolute dependence of the Dene on their terrain since time immemorial. An anonymous writer in the *Saskatchewan Indian Cultural Centre Newsletter* states, "The Denesuliné have a special relationship with their traditional territories and identify themselves by reference to those lands. . . . It is on the Barren lands where the Caribou are most plentiful. . . . This land [has always been used] as their hunting, trapping and fishing territories" (1994b: n.p.). Ac-cordingly, singing the songs can reconfirm this close connection through their linguistic references to its beautiful pink rocks, intermixed with muskeg, boreal forest, and numerous lakes and rivers. For the Dene, the land, Mother Earth, is life itself. If life is to continue, the land must be cared for (Tatti et al. 1993a: 27).

Similarly, singing love songs can reconfirm the social values of the Dene as well as help to increase the self-confidence of the individual concerned. The basis of Dene society is respect for the elders. This is linked to the importance of getting along in groups when circumstances may be difficult through lack of ready food, severe weather conditions, or scarcity of shelter and means of transportation. In such situations the ability to express humor may be a very important survival tactic indeed. Friendship is highly valued and according to Dene custom involves love, kindness, trust, and respect. Friends teach one another, practice things together, help one another, and share thoughts, ideas, and things. The ideal was to try to develop friendships with all people, whereas the worst crime for the Dene was to deny food to another person (Tatti et al. 1993b: xxxvii, 172, 200).

Conclusion

What the Dene feel can be accomplished through listening to, learning, and performing these songs is the meaning of symbols that through the Dene culture over a long period of time have become entwined with important values and signifying practices of that culture. The articulation of these songs comes from the Dene people, but at the same time these songs express essential identities of the Dene. In other words, the Dene elders have been able to state directly what has become obscured in Western society, the values that are expressed through music.

In order to fully understand a Dogrib Dene personal song, Lucy Lafferty stresses that a person should know the circumstances of its origin. It is on that primary level that these songs express fully the identity of the Dogrib Dene. However, these songs can speak very powerfully to Dogrib persons who have not had the opportunity to hear these songs in context or do not speak the language. Christine Allen-Doctor is a Dogrib speaker living intermittently "in the South." Her first reaction to hearing recordings of love and land songs was queries about the singers and who would have recorded these songs to be played out of context. With her daughter Cindy Allen, who does not speak Dogrib, she found that "the voices of the singers conveyed feeling and depth which seemed almost otherworldly in nature and performance." Cindy further stated, "It seemed to me that the singers' voices carried words which wanted to be heard into the far reaches of the universe. The hymns also seemed to be private in nature and possibly only for the singer and the recipient, whoever or whatever it was intended for. I thought I was eavesdropping, but at the same time I felt privileged to listen to these hymns" (personal communication, 1996). One can make observations on the connotative level such as those above by Elaine Keillor, but only a person who has been fully involved in the economic, social, political, and climatic factors of life as a Dogrib Dene can interlink these two levels fully (Blaukopf 1992: 269).

Notes

1. J. Alden Mason made some cylinder recordings of Dene songs in 1913–15, whereas Elaine Keillor made field trips to Denendeh in 1984, 1987, 1994, and 1995.

2. Nicole Beaudry has given the term *ets'sula* of North Slavey with an English translation of "personal pleasure songs" (1992: 87).

3. Victorine Mercredi, a Chipewyan, reports that "the Chipewyan used to drum and stand dancing in the same place. . . . [W]hen finally they were with the Cree people, they started to dance in a circle" (Sutherland 1991: 117).

4. Examples of these dance songs are recorded on *Chief Jimmy Bruneau School Drummers: Drum Dance Music of the Dogrib* (Canyon CR-16260, 1993).

References

Abel, Kerry. 1993. *Drum Songs: Glimpses of Dene History.* Montreal: McGill-Queen's University Press.

Beaudry, Nicole. 1992. "The Language of Dreams: Songs of the Dene Indians (Canada)." *World of Music: Journal of the International Institute for Traditional Music* 34, no. 2: 72–90.

Blaukopf, Kurt. 1992. *Musical Life in a Changing Society.* Rev. ed. Portland, Ore.: Amadeus Press, 1992.

Blondin, George. 1990. *When the World Was New: Stories of the Sahtú Dene.* Yellowknife, Northwest Territories: Outcrop.

Helm, J., and N. O. Lurie. 1966. *The Dogrib Hand Game.* National Museum of Canada Bulletin 205, Anthropological Series 71. Ottawa: National Museum of Canada.

Keillor, Elaine. 1986. "The Role of Dogrib Youth in the Continuation of Their Musical Traditions." *Yearbook for Traditional Music* 18: 61–76.

McGee, W. F., and Paul Merkley. 1991. "A Real-Time Logarithmic-Frequency Phase Vocorder." *Computer Music Journal* 15, no. 1: 20–27.

Moore, Pat, and Angela Wheelock, eds. 1990. *Wolverine Myths and Visions: Dene Traditions from Northern Alberta.* Edmonton: University of Alberta Press.

Rogers, Jimmie N. 1989. *The Country Music Message: Revisited.* Fayetteville: University of Arkansas Press.

Ryan, Joan. 1995. *Doing Things the Right Way.* Calgary: University of Calgary Press / Arctic Institute of North America.

Saskatchewan Indian Cultural Centre Newsletter. 1994a. "Dene Culture." (August): 13–14.

———. 1994b. "Denesuliné Land Claims beyond 60th Parallel." (April): n.p.

Sutherland, Agnes. 1991. *Living Kindness: The Memoirs of Madeleine Bird with Agnes Sutherland*. Yellowknife, Northwest Territories: Outcrop.

Tatti, Fibbie, with J. C. Catholique, Lucy Lafferty, Rosa Mantla, Philip Mackenzie, Andy Norwegian, Fanny Swarzentruber, and Mitsu Oishi. 1993a. *Dene Kede Curriculum Document: Grades K–6*. With elders George Blondin, Mary Firth Sr., Judith Drybone Catholic, Joe Boucher, Bella Drymeat Ross, Elizabeth Chocolate Mackenzie, Joseph Jerome Bonnetronge, Marie Cadieux, Adele Hardisty, and Alphonse Eronchi. Yellowknife, Canada: Northwest Territories Education Development Branch.

———. 1993b. *Dene Kede Curriculum Teacher's Resource Manual: Grades K–6*. Yellowknife, Canada: Northwest Territories Education, Culture, and Employment.

3

The Story of Dirty Face
Power and Song in Western
Washington Coast Salish
Myth Narratives

LAUREL SERCOMBE

Stories and songs have been part of the rich cultural life of Pacific Northwest indigenous communities for many generations. Storytellers in traditional and contemporary contexts entertain and instruct both children and adults by evoking a lively world of characters, places, and events. Their narratives tell the history of a people, demonstrate cultural values and concepts of humor and beauty, and transmit important spiritual information.

Among the Coast Salish people of western Washington State, the formal telling of myth narratives was traditionally a seasonal event, taking place mainly in the winter months. The disruption of lifeways caused by white settlement in the mid-nineteenth century, accompanied by the dispersion of village settlements and the removal of children to government schools, also affected the cycle of seasonal storytelling. By the late nineteenth century, anthropologists and linguists had begun collecting stories and song texts from elders around western Washington in the belief that they were documenting cultures that would soon be extinct. With the advent of recorded sound media such as the cylinder recorder, they were able to document the *sound* of songs, not just the texts; even so, spoken narratives continued to be transcribed mainly by hand.

Among the stories and story fragments collected, many are actually short episodes of lengthy Coast Salish epic narratives, in particular the account of the world before human beings came to live in it. At some point during this mythic era, the world is transformed by a Changer or Transformer figure, known to Lushootseed (Puget Salish) speakers in the Puget Sound region of western Washington as *dkʷiibəa* (see table 3.1 for a guide to the pronunciation of the Puget Salish words in this essay). Through a series of encounters with the animal-people who live there, the Transformer changes them and the physical world to the form we know today, each being becoming associated with a particular location (Miller 1999b: 50). Stories were placed geographically where things had happened in myth times, charging those places and resident spirit beings with profound psychic and spiritual importance in the human community. The myths taught and reinforced ideas about the spirit world, which was believed to exist parallel to the human world, and the human world at an earlier time before human beings arrived on the scene.

Myth narratives are a special category of Lushootseed oral litera-ture; northern speakers called them *syəhúb* (or *syəyəhúb*), and southern speakers called them *sxʷiʔa'b*. Other categories are historical accounts,

Table 3.1. Guide to Lushootseed pronunciation

Lushootseed Term	Pronunication	English Translation
čəbəš	chebásh	misty rain
dúkʷibəł	dókwibelh	Changer; the being who changed the world to its present form
łəcəb	lhetseb	heavy mist prior to a rain
łəltəb	lhelteb	sprinkle, mist
qəlb	qelb	rain
qəlbəxʷ	qelbewh	It's starting to rain.
səlus	seloos	junco
siʔab	si'ab	honored one; high-class person
slahal	slahal	bone game, hand game
spicxʷ	spitswh	"Dirty Face"; one of the animal people, later transformed into a small dark-headed bird by the Changer
stoblə	stoble	north wind
sxʷiʔa'b	shwi'a'b	myth narrative (southern Lushootseed)
syəhúb / syəyəhúb	syehób / syeyehób	myth narrative (northern Lushootseed)
tebt'a'b	t'ebt'a'b	wren
xwa'xwai / xwaxwe	wha'whai / whawhi	a bird similar to the junco
xʷəlšucid	whelshootsid	Lushootseed
yəlab / yəla'b	yeláb / yela'b	uncle or aunt of either parent when that parent is deceased; parent; forebearer
yəl'yəla'b	yel'yela'b	parents; relatives; ancestors

Table 3.1. (cont.)

Normalized Symbol	Phonetic Symbol	Words Illustrating Approximate Pronunciation
a	[a]	the "o" in "hot"
ə	[ə]	the "u" in "but"
ch	[č]	the "ch" in "child"
gw	[gʷ]	no English equivalent; like "gw" with the lips rounded
h̲	[x̌]	no English equivalent; a raspy "h" sound like the "ch" in German "ich"; said deep in the throat
hw	[xʷ]	no English equivalent; like the "wh" in "which" with the lips rounded
h̲w	[x̌ʷ]	no English equivalent; like "*h*" with the lips rounded
i	[i]	the "ee" in "feed"; sometimes pronounced like the "a" in "fake"
k	[k]	the "k" in "kiss"
kw	[kʷ]	the "qu" in "quick"
l'	[l̓]	no English equivalent; similar to the "l" in "feel" with a glottal stop
lh	[ł]	no English equivalent; barred "l"; like the sound between the "c" and the "lay" in "clay" if the word is drawn out
o	[u]	the "o" in "note"; sometimes pronounced "oo" as in "boot"
q	[q]	like "k" but with back of the tongue raised against the back roof of the mouth
s	[s]	the "s" in "sit"
sh	[š]	the "sh" in "shoe"
t'	[t']	no English equivalent; like the "t" in "vote" with a glottal stop
ts	[c]	no English equivalent; the "ts" in "cats"
'	[ʔ,']	glottal stop; like the pause in "uh-oh"

personal reports, and nontraditional stories (Bates, Hess, and Hilbert 1994: 360).

This study focuses on *syəhúb/sxʷiʔa'b* about Dirty Face and the song that is an integral part of the narrative. Dirty Face, or *spicxʷ* (pronounced *spits* with a soft *wh* at the end) is shown to have features that clearly identify it as Coast Salish and, more specifically, as indigenous to the Puget Sound region, probably originating among Lushootseed speakers. I will provide an illustration of the ways in which myth narratives reveal indigenous cultural and spiritual values by looking closely at the primacy of place in myth narratives, the ways stories provide instruction in appropriate social behavior, and the role and significance of myth narrative songs in spiritual practice. By comparing ten recordings of Dirty Face's song by different storytellers, I will address this question: What makes different versions of a song the same song? That is, what gives a song its integrity as a distinct musical utterance?

Geographical Setting

The Northwest coast—encompassing the coastal groups of Alaska, British Columbia, Washington, and Oregon—was identified as an indigenous cultural area by late-nineteenth-century ethnographers. In addition to shared geographical and cultural features are striking differences. Thirteen entirely different language families are represented. Within these families are twenty-three Salishan languages, sixteen of which are spoken by coastal groups and seven by interior groups (Thompson and Kinkade 1990: 33). Coast Salish speakers occupy areas of western British Columbia and Washington and a small section of northwestern Oregon. The focus for this essay is the Puget Sound region of western Washington and the oral narrative traditions of Lushootseed (or xʷəlšucid, also known as Puget Salish) and the neighboring languages of Twana, Clallam, Samish, Lummi, Quinault, Upper and Lower Chehalis, and Cowlitz.

Coast Salish Songs

As is generally true for North American indigenous groups, songs, or sung utterances, constitute musical expression for Coast Salish people. Solo or group songs are often accompanied by sound instruments. At the time of first contact (and still in use today) were drums (both idiophones, such as box drums, and membranophones, such as frame drums) and many types of rattles (including scallop-shell rattles, deer-hoof rattles, and wooden vessel rattles). Though today it is common to hear the unaccompanied "Native American" flute at gatherings in the Pacific Northwest, the flute was not used as a melodic instrument there until the late twentieth century.

Coast Salish songs may be received spiritually, inherited, or composed by individuals and performed individually or by groups of singers, depending on the kind of song and performance context. They are usually accompanied by drums or rattles or both and, often, by dancing. All ceremonial activities, including those of the winter dance season, potlatches, and welcoming, naming, and First Salmon ceremonies, include both songs and dance. Singing is also central to social activities, such as the gambling game *slahal.*

Spiritual power is believed to be at the basis of all songs, but not all songs are equally spiritually charged. Coast Salish religious practice centers around the individual acquisition of a spirit power through questing or other means. Spirit power manifests as a song that stays with a person for life. The onset of illness in the winter months is a signal to the individual that his or her power wants to be danced. During the winter season, spirit dancers "dance their songs" in the smokehouse, witnessed and supported by members of the community who drum and sing along with the dancer. This public demonstration is required for proper maintenance of the relationship with one's power. In contemporary Coast Salish communities the range of musical activities and interests is much like those of any other community in the United States or Canada, but the older indigenous song practices continue to operate in both public and private domains.

Oral Literature and Myth Narratives

In contemporary usage, "oral literature(s)" suggests narrative forms of expression that are or have been primarily shared and transmitted orally and, because they are "told," may be considered performances of verbal art. It is used here to refer to the narrative forms associated with precontact Coast Salish life, including myths and tales, historical accounts, personal narratives, and formal oratory, such as speeches. Stories—including myths, tales, legends, histories, and personal narratives—are distinguished from oratory, and myths or myth narratives *(syəhúb/syəyəhúb)* are distinguished from other stories by their cultural centrality and their setting in "a world that is different from or earlier than the one in which the myth is related" (Farrer 1997: 576). A definition emphasizing indigenous meaning has been suggested by Jarold Ramsey: "Myths are sacred traditional stories whose shaping function is to tell the people who know them who they are; how, through what origins and transformations, they have come to possess their particular world; and how they should live in that world, and with each other" (1999: 6).

Myth narratives are also distinct from other stories in their placement of humans "between a world in the process of being transformed and prepared for the coming of human beings and a world rendered meaningful and spiritually potent inhabited by human beings. It is a distinction between mythic beings endowed with significance and potency and humans seeking that endowment. The mythic world necessarily precedes yet continues to reverberate through the world of tales" (Frey and Hymes 1998: 587).

Finally, myth narratives happen on a special temporal plane; in "narrative time" events happen in relation to transformative stages of history, such as the coming of the Changer or Transformer figure (Wiget 1985: 4). That figure "mediates" time so that the world may be understood in seemingly contradictory ways. Susie Sampson Peter, a Skagit (Coast Salish) storyteller and historian, embodies this ability to mediate between historical and mythic time when she uses the word *dkʷiibəa* (changer) to describe collector Leon Metcalf in the early 1950s, in a passage translated from Skagit: "Yet I remember the old ways and I will ever recall them because now this Boston [American white person] has come to us, this changer who wishes to know all about these other things" (Hilbert in Hilbert and Miller 1995: 13).

The Story of Dirty Face, or *spicxʷ:* "The Man Who Would Not Wash His Face"

> Dirty Face lives with his wife's family, and it is his job to bring in the wood. This work causes his face to become increasingly dirty, and he is criticized and told repeatedly by his in-laws to wash it. At first he refuses to wash his face, but finally he reluctantly agrees. He goes to the river and turns toward his own relations to the south, telling them in a song that he has been asked to wash his face. This appeal results immediately in the arrival of the south wind and rain. The mountain snow melts, and the world floods, destroying everything.

The story of Dirty Face, or *spicxʷ*, takes place in the myth or epic era, before the arrival of *dúibəł*. It features Dirty Face, a young man harassed by his wife's family because of his dirty or sooty face. His appearance resembles that of a small bird with a dark gray or brown hood or facial markings whose form Dirty Face takes after the world is changed. He is identified as Snowbird in several renditions (Henry Allen, Jerry Kanim) but also as Thrush (Peter Heck, Mary Iley), Wren (Frank Allen), Snipe (Lizzie Martin), Oregon Junco (Emma Conrad), Ground Sparrow or Swamp Sparrow (Joe Young [Puyallup], who says specifically in Marian Smith's notes that *spicxʷ* is not Junco, "a bird similar to the Oregon junco, the common name of which . . . is *xwa'xwai* or *xwaxwə*" [Jonah Jack, interpreter, cited in Ballard 1929: 49]), or generically as a little gray bird with dark rings around his eyes (Ann Jack). In Emma Conrad's version the character is called *səlus*, Lushootseed for Junco, rather than *spicxʷ*. He may have been associated with different birds depending on the home of the storyteller and the winter birds in residence.

spicxʷ is told throughout the Puget Sound region of western Washington State. I have located fourteen versions in various published and unpublished sources and ten recordings of the song that accompanies the story. Despite their differences, they have in common what Upper Skagit elder Vi Hilbert calls the "backbone" of the story. Among these different versions, only four renderings include both the story and its song recorded as a cohesively performed unit. In the remaining cases, story and song are displaced from one another for a variety of reasons (see the Appendix for the list of story and song versions).

spicx^w is not a discrete, autonomous story but rather an episode within the Lushootseed epic narrative that describes the coming of *dk^wiibəa*, the Transformer. *spicx^w* is part of a Lushootseed cast of characters that includes Bluejay, Raven, Crow, North Wind, South Wind, and many others. To the cultural insider, these characters and their personalities are well known, and their appearance in a *syəhúb/syəyəhúb* carries with it a whole set of associations. The narrative account of *spicx^w* and his problems with his in-laws may be told on its own, or it may lead into a version of the epic describing the big flood and its aftermath, as Annie Daniels's version does. *spicx^w* also appears in other stories where he plays a supporting, rather than leading, role.

Locating the Dirty Face Story in Lushootseed Culture

The story of Dirty Face, or *spicx^w*, illustrates the importance of place in western Washington Coast Salish narratives. The following local references and other features of the various story and song versions clearly identify it as Coast Salish and, more specifically, as indigenous to the Puget Sound region, probably originating among southern Lushootseed speakers.

First, the use of a culturally significant pattern number in some versions helps to localize the story world. The pattern number five was dominant among the southern Lushootseed, southwestern Coast Salish, and groups in western Oregon. In one version, *spicx^w* is married to one of five sisters and has four brothers-in-law (Snuqualmi Charlie); in two versions *spicx^w* is told five times to wash his face (Snyder 1968: [Jerry Kanim]; Adamson 1934: 1 [Peter Heck]).

Second, in several versions Dirty Face is associated with a specific location. In Peter Heck's Upper Chehalis version Muskrat dives for dirt five times (the pattern number again) to re-create the world after the flood brought on by Thrush. Muskrat names the resulting mound of land Tiger Lily *(masi'ak' 'i)*, now called Black Mountain (located near Gate in Upper Chehalis country) (Adamson 1934: 1–2). Jonas Secena's Upper Chehalis rendering also locates Black Mountain as the place Muskrat created with the aid of his spirit power; he adds that at Gate (near the Mima Prairie) "the earth still remains in the shape of waves" (Adamson 1934: 3).

In a version of the Star Husband myth narrative, *spicx^w (tebt'a'b)* (Wren) successfully rescues the Star Child and is told by the Transformer to stay at Snoqualmie Pass, where the story took place. "And they told *spicxʷ* 'You're going to stay with the Snoqualmie now. Your name is Snoqualmie now' ... And there are lots of *spicxʷ*, in that country right today" (Elmendorf 1961: 27, 30). (This version was told by Twana speaker Frank Allen, who got the story from Snoqualmie Doctor Jack.)

Third, the Lushootseed term *yəlab* is present in most of the versions for which we have story or song text in the original language, and the concept is central to understanding the story. *Yelab* may refer specifically to an uncle or aunt when the parent is deceased, or more generally to relatives or ancestors (Bates, Hess, and Hilbert 1994: 277). In most renditions Dirty Face goes to the river and addresses his own relations to the South, his *yəla'b* or *yəl'yəla'b*, to complain about his in-laws and ask for assistance. He does so in the form of a song, in which he tells them he has been asked to wash his face. The seriousness of this request is clear, as his plea is answered instantly in the form of rain and wind, resulting in dire consequences that, at one level, avenge his poor treatment.

The theme of family roles and especially relations between affines (those related by marriage) dominates the story of Dirty Face. In his wife's family's household, he does the dirty work of bringing in the firewood, a lowly job usually reserved for women or slaves, and is criticized by his in-laws. The practice of village exogamy (marriage outside one's group) and its dynamics are reflected in the situation of Dirty Face. In most versions his people are different from his wife's people: he is from the Southwind, Southwest Wind, or Rain-Wind people; in one version his wife is specifically contrasted as being from the North Wind people (Henry Allen). It was not unusual in the Puget Sound region for a man to live with his wife's family, and Dirty Face does so in most versions. In Jerry Kanim's telling, however, Dirty Face lives with his relatives (there is no mention of his wife) and appeals to his nephew South Wind (who calls him *yala'ps*); Dirty Face then warns his own *yalyala'ps*, the elk, to head for the hills to avoid the coming flood. In Ann Jack's sketchy version family dynamics are altogether absent; it is his neighbors who tell Dirty Face to wash, after which it begins to rain. And in the Upper Chehalis telling by Jonas Secena, Dirty Face is Thrush, a female disgraced among her people for not washing or bathing.

And fourth, though the *syəhúb/sxʷiʔa'b* about Dirty Face appears throughout the northern and southern Lushootseed, Twana, and Upper Chehalis–speaking areas, the songs in all seven versions documented here have texts in Lushootseed. Its close association with the Lushootseed myth world and geographical landmarks associated with the work of *dúibəɫ*, the Lushootseed Changer, strongly suggest a Lushootseed origin.

Dirty Face as a Teaching Tool

The story of Dirty Face, or *spicx*^w, undoubtedly served a pedagogical function at one time, providing instruction about appropriate ways to behave in families and in the community as well as introducing elements of esoteric knowledge and spiritual practice. For example, cleanliness is one of the central themes in the story of *spicx*^w, with his dirty face and refusal to wash that ignites family tensions. The importance of personal hygiene is a message children have heard for many generations in Coast Salish communities: "Young [Nooksack] children from the age of five or six years were brought up in a tradition of personal cleanliness and self-discipline. Daily bathing in the river was the cornerstone of this regime" (Amoss 1978: 13).

In the case of Dirty Face, however, the insistence on cleanliness appears to backfire, since by washing he brings on cataclysmic destruction. Clearly, the world as constituted in the story was not operating properly and had to be cleared away in the anticipation of re-creation, making the conflict between Dirty Face and his in-laws appearing to be about more than personal hygiene. He is different from them and considered lower class, but he knows what they ask of him is wrong. As Henry Allen tells it, "He is just a black cloud, that South Wind [Snowbird]; he shouldn't wash his face. His duty is black cloud and lots of rain" (Elmendorf 1961: 104).

Ultimately, Dirty Face must do what his wife's family wishes, and it is at this point in the story that a crucial transition is made from the mundane world of the animal-people to that of supernatural power. Washing takes on ritual meaning, suggestive of the ritual preparations for real-life spirit acquisition: "The passage from the human sphere to the nonhuman sphere was ritually dangerous and hedged with taboos. Contact could be achieved only if the human supplicant were purged of the taint of human existence. Bathing cleaned off the smell of sweat and the odor of smoke from the plank houses" (Amoss 1978: 13).

The Relationship between Myth Narrative Songs and Spirit Power Songs

The story of Dirty Face shows how myth narratives may demonstrate the relationship between the Coast Salish individual and his or her spirit power. Though it may not be explicit in every rendition, action in myth narratives is often brought about by a character calling on his or her spirit power by invoking his or her song. From time to time the results are humorous, particularly when a character's power proves too weak to effect the desired action, or when it is clear to other myth characters that the character has only a simulation of power. In the case of Dirty Face, the strength of his spirit power is revealed in a song potent enough to destroy the world (of course, after his dramatic achievement, accomplished with the assistance of his power, he is unceremoniously turned into a bird with no such power).

If myth characters mirror their modern human counterparts in calling on their spirit powers for assistance, how do the power songs of these myth characters relate to actual spirit-power songs? Because such songs are associated with spiritual power, their appearance in a myth narrative alerts the listener to the proximity of power in some form. A song may be introduced in the story as the power song of the character singing, or the circumstances of the story may suggest that it is, but no accounts suggest that these are real power songs. They do appear to imitate actual power songs, and it is likely that myth-world spirit dancing provided an introduction to the activities of the winter dance season to small children not yet allowed in the smokehouse. Toby Langen suggests that many myth power songs are parodies of the real thing. In the Lushootseed story "Crow Is Sick," Langen's commentary reveals the entire story as a parody of the onset of sickness that leads to one's first spirit dance; both Raven's and Crow's songs are used inappropriately in terms of expected behaviors and thus appear to be parodies (in Bierwert 1996: 136–39).

Parody power songs may also imitate the esoteric language found in real power songs. Vi Hilbert found the *spicx* song of Annie Daniels to be untranslatable; the only word that comes through undisguised is yəl'yəla'b, the ancestors to whom he appeals for help. It is clear from the versions of the song of Dirty Face compiled for this study that everyday speech has been altered in a number of ways in the creation of sung text. Langen (in Bierwert 1996: 136–39) and Snyder (1968: 50) have also documented alterations in language in Lushootseed stories.

The Relationship between Myth Narrative Songs and Sung Ritual Words (Enchantments)

When Dirty Face invokes the rain and wind, he is using the power of language, in this case sung language, to directly effect action. This kind of demonstration suggests an alternative interpretation to that of power-song parody. Another kind of power comes from "family wisdom" possessed and controlled by high-ranking families in precontact Coast Salish communities (and still operating in some forms). Among the kinds of esoteric knowledge they controlled were ritual words or enchantments used to control animals, weather spirits, and humans (Miller 1999b: 91). Spoken or sung "formulas" to change the weather appear to be a special category of esoteric language among Puget Sound–area people. The ability to change the weather goes along with being *siʔab*, or high class, in Lushootseed myth times (Langen and Barthold 1991: 4).

The power of language and other ritual performance to bridge the myth world and the everyday world is confirmed by tellers of the Dirty Face story. Tom Milroy (Puyallup) told Arthur Ballard that if the story were told, it would bring rain; Joe Young (Puyallup) said that if *spicxʷ* is seen taking a bath on a sunny day and looking south, it will rain (1929: 50). Henry Allen told William Elmendorf the *spicxʷ* story and then commented, "When North Wind comes here in winter time we sing these songs. We catch Snowbird and kill him and burn him in a fire and sing for *čəbaš čəbaš čəbaš*. Then the icicles melt and wet, warm weather comes. When they do this they think of this story. They go outdoors and call *vəbaš* three times to change the weather. I can remember people doing this" (1961: 105).

Dirty Face shares certain features with stories concerning the contest between the North Wind and South (or Chinook, Storm, or Rain) Wind; in fact, they seem to be conflated at times. In the telling of "North Wind and Storm Wind" told by Dan Silelus, *stoblə* (North Wind) has defeated the Chinook Wind people, leaving only a young man and his grandmother. The young man gradually gains strength (ritually prepares for and acquires spirit power) in order to defeat *stoblə*. As his power becomes stronger, he tells his grandmother to wash her face (which has been fouled by *stoblə*'s slave, Raven), and her washing brings on the rain and warmer weather. In this case there is no song; the ritual washing is enough to bring the rain. There may or may not have been a song at that point in the story at one time, but it is clear that some ritual action is necessary to mark the boundary between the everyday and the spiritual.

What Makes a Song a Song? Comparing Versions of the Song of Dirty Face

If the various versions of the Dirty Face story all share the same "backbone," we would expect to find it in the song of Dirty Face, too. In table 3.2 linguistic, musical, and performance data about the ten song renditions have been organized for easy comparison (my transcriptions of the ten versions were the source of this data; see musical example 3.1 for a transcription of the Annie Daniels rendition, included here as an example).

The ten renditions of the song have a core similarity that is not always obvious. None of the ten versions are identical, musically or textually (including the three by Henry Allen). Of the ten, three have primarily triple

Table 3.2. Comparison of songs in the *spicxʷ* story (arranged by transcription number)

#	Singer Name	Language of Singer	Language of Song	Language of Story	Meter	Pulse (bpm)	Range (Sem./Int.)	# of Tones	Rhythmic Accomp.
1	A. Daniels	Duwamish (S.L.)	Duwamish (S.L.)	Duwamish (S.L.)	variable	48–60	7/P5	4	none
2	L. Martin	Lummi	Skagit (N.L.)?	English	duple	104–108	7/P5	3	none
3	M. Lamont	Snohomish (N.L.)	Lushootseed	—	variable	60–84	7/P5	4	none
4	J. Kanim	Snoqualmie (S.L.)	Snoqualmie?(S.L.)	Snoqualmie?(S.L.)	unmetered	ca. 48	7/P5	4	none
5	J. Kanim	Snoqualmie (S.L.)	Snoqualmie?(S.L.)	Snoqualmie?(S.L.)	variable	60	7/P5	4	none
6	J. Stillman	Snoqualmie (S.L.)	Snoqualmie?(S.L.)	—	unmetered	—	7/P5	3	none
7	H. Allen	Twana	Lushootseed (S.)	English	triple	40–48	7/P5	4	none
8	H. Allen	Twana	Lushootseed (S.)	—	triple	52	7/P5	4	none
9	H. Allen	Twana	Lushootseed (S.)	—	triple	52	7/P5	3	none
10	M. Davis	Upper Chehalis	Lushootseed (S.)	—	duple	58	2/M2	2	none

#	Singer Name	Characteristic Rhythm	Characteristic Interval	Contour	Pitch Change	Vocal Quality	Volume	Audience
1	A. Daniels	/ u	M2	undulating	slight drop	open; no pulsing; slight tremolo	soft-medium	no
2	L. Martin	u /	m3	undulating	slight fluctuation	ditto; no tremolo	medium	yes
3	M. Lamont	u / u /	m3/M3	undulating	none	ditto; no tremolo	soft-medium	no
4	J. Kanim	u /	m3	undulating	none	ditto; slight tremolo	medium	no
5	J. Kanim	—	M2	undulating	none	ditto; slight tremolo	medium	no
6	J. Stillman	—	M2	undulating	some indistinct pitches	ditto; no tremolo	soft-medium	no
7	H. Allen	u /	m3	undulating	none	ditto; no tremolo	soft-medium	no
8	H. Allen	u /	unison	undulating	none	ditto; no tremolo	soft-medium	no
9	H. Allen	u /	m3/M3	undulating	none	ditto; no tremolo	soft-medium	no
10	M. Davis	/ u	M2	und. (narrow)	+ 1 semitone	ditto; no tremolo	loud	no

Musical example 3.1. Transcription of the "Song of Dirty Face" as sung by Annie Daniels (1954). Transcribed by Laurel Sercombe.

meter (all three Henry Allen versions); two have primarily duple meter; three have variable meter (tending toward duple); and two have free meter (one tending toward duple). Pulse tends to be fairly slow, ranging between forty and sixty quarter notes per minute, with two examples extending outside that range. Melodic range is a fifth for all but one version, and most contain three or four scale tones. The characteristic, or most commonly occurring, interval is the third (m3 for three versions and both m3 and M3 for two) or the major second (four versions) (in one version a characteristic interval could not be identified). All share an undulating melodic contour.

What unifies these renditions musically has primarily to do with rhythmic patterns and the interrelationship of rhythm and text. To demonstrate this interrelationship, transcriptions of the song texts are presented; they have been compiled from a number of different sources, and orthographic differences have been preserved. Some text has been altered from spoken form, and meaning is often obscured. I have had assistance with the transcriptions and translations of several versions; the names of the text transcriber and translator appear to the right of the first lines of text for each. Texts are arranged by name of raconteur. It has already been mentioned that every recorded version of the song of Dirty Face is sung in Lushootseed (probably all southern). This includes the three renditions by Henry Allen (Twana/Skokomish), one by Marion Davis (Upper Chehalis), and one by Lizzie Martin (Lummi) from neighboring areas:

1) Annie Daniels (southern Lushootseed—Duwamish) (Vi Hilbert/Toby C. S. Langen)
    A [sung] *buləb, buləs ʔaš tədi*
        [vocables?]
    B [sung] *hagʷəxʷ c'əd ʔuyəq̓əq̓ʔəq̓ʷus [ʔ] yəl̓yəl̓ab [ʔ] ʔkʷ*
        (For a long time I . . . speak up . . . face . . . my
        uncles/relatives)
    A [sung] *buləb, buləs ʔaš tədi*
        [vocables?]
    B1 [sung] *hagʷəxʷ c'əd ʔuyəq̓əq̓ʔəq̓ʷus [ʔ] ʔi*
        (For a long time I . . . speak up . . . face . . . yes)
        [x̌əl̓x̌əl̓təd ʔiiiiiʔ]? [not translatable]
    [spoken] *huy gʷəlqəlbəxʷ gʷəlqəlbəxʷ gʷəlqəlbəxʷ*
    gʷəlqəlbəxʷ gʷəlqəl
        (And then it rained and rained and rained . . .)

2) Lizzie Martin (Lushootseed—Skagit?) (my transcription)
    A [sung] *ʔuhilitəb ca'd*
    B [sung] *l̓ayaqʷyaqʷo-*
    B1 [sung] *yaqʷyaqʷo-*
    C [sung] *yə'lyəla'b*

3) Martha Lamont (southern Lushootseed) (Thom Hess)
    A [sung] *ʔucutəb čəd aədxʷyəq̓yəq̓usəbəd šə dyalyalab*
    sq̓ʷəul̓gʷədxʷ
    B [sung] *čabəs čabəs q̓ʷul̓gʷədxʷ*
    B [sung] *čabəs čabəs q̓ʷul̓gʷədxʷ*

4) Jerry Kanim, no. 1 (southern Lushootseed—Snoqualmie)
(Warren Snyder)
    A [sung] *toco'tb čad łatxʷya'qaqyaqo'sbd ə*
        (I was told to wash my face. Yes.)
    B [sung] *ło?'a(ya)ƛ̓axʷčaxʷ stgʷa'q̓ʷ*
        (You will come now, South Wind.)

5) Jerry Kanim, no. 2 (southern Lushootseed—Snoqualmie)
(Warren Snyder)
     A [sung] *ta'ta'q̓tcotłə dya'lyalap*
       (Go up into the mountains my uncles, the elk.)
     B [sung] *otxʷya'qaqyaqo'sbaxʷ cəd (i)*
       (I wash my face.)

6) Jack Stillman (southern Lushootseed—Snoqualmie) (Arthur
Ballard)
     A [sung] *t'a-'tAq̓ttsutłi t'a-'tAq̓ttsutłi cIdya-'lyala-B*
       (Move back from the river, my uncles)
     B [sung] *utxʷwiya'q̓aq̓iya'q̓o'sIbaxtcId cIdya-lyala-'B*
       (I am going to wash my face, my uncles)

7–9) Henry Allen (southern Lushootseed) (all three renditions)
(William Elmendorf)
     A [sung] *oco'təbča'd łəyə'q̓ʷyaq̓ʷ o'səbəd*
       (They tell me to wash my face)
     B [sung] *šdəyə'lyəla'b sk'əxʷo'lgʷadə'xʷ*
       (O my uncles from the South Wind World.)
     C [spoken] *čəbə'š čəbə'š čəbə'š*
       (Wet drizzle, wet drizzle, wet drizzle)

10) Marion Davis (southern Lushootseed) (my transcription)
     A [sung] . . . *i* . . . *oco'təbča'd* . . . *yə'lyəla'b* . . .
     B [sung] [?]
     A/A1? [sung] . . . *i* . . . *oco'təbča'd* . . . *yə'lyəla'b* . . .
     B or B1? [sung]

The rhythmic patterns of these songs are characterized generally by repeated triplet or dotted rhythmic figures (short-long-short or long-short-long), often difficult to differentiate. These rhythms may be accompanied in the text by repeated words (or vocables), reduplicated or altered forms of words, or text strings that convey lexically cohesive statements. I propose that it is the word *yəla'b*, found in some form in nine versions of the story, that provides the rhythmic foundation for the song.

The internal rhythm of the singular form *yəláb* (short-long) or the plural *yə'lyəláb* (long-short-long) is reinforced by the use of the word *vəbə'š* (short-long), glossed as "mist," in southern Lushootseed (Bates, Hess, and Hilbert 1994: 62), and also translated descriptively by William Elmendorf as "wet drizzle" in several versions. In all three of Henry Allen's renditions it appears as a repeated spoken word at the end of the song—*čabə'š čabə'š čabə'š*—in the rhythm "short-long [pause] short-long [pause] short-long," with emphasis on the long underlined syllable. In the Annie Daniels version the song is followed by the spoken line—*huy gʷəlqəlbəxʷ gʷəlqəlbəxʷ gʷəlqəlbəxʷ gʷəlqəlbəxʷ gʷəlqəl* (And then it rained and rained and rained . . .)—with the repeated syllables arranged in even triplets with a pulse on *qelb* (rain) each time (*qəlbəxʷ* is northern Lushootseed for "It's starting to rain") (Bates, Hess, and Hilbert 1994: 175). These ending phrases have both onomatopoeic and chantlike qualities. *Vəbəs* also appears in Lamont's version in sung form, where it is repeated within the phrase and again in a repeat of the entire text phrase. No versions use the words *aacəb* (southern Lushootseed) (heavy mist prior to a general rain) or *aaltəb* (sprinkle, mist), perhaps because they have an accent on the first syllable and thus violate the underlying rhythmic principle of the song.

The rhythmic pattern embodied by the words *yəla'b* and *čabə'š* is evident throughout this body of songs, even where the words themselves do not appear. Vocables with the same rhythm may substitute, as with *buləb, buləs* in the Daniels version.

Conclusion

Each myth narrative performance, whether to a gathering of hearth mates, an anthropologist with a tape recorder, or a hall full of students, is a ritual reenactment or re-creation of the mythic world. No two performed events are ever exactly the same, but it is that linkage that matters and that results each time in a "new re-creation" (Regna Darnell in Silver and Miller 1997: 130). The presence of songs within myth narratives signals a communicative shift, alerting the listener to the proximity of power or the knowledge of power, moving the event into a spiritual frame. Although the fragmentary record we have of the song of *spicxʷ* tells us little about the history of its performance, from what we do know we may at least conjecture that the rhythmic patterns and interrelationship of rhythm and text described here are the primary means by which the song has been identified and remembered for generations. When the human and spirit worlds are thus linked in song, storytellers and listeners alike recognize the power of that evocation.

Acknowledgments

I would like to acknowledge Thom Hess, Vi Hilbert, Toby Langen, and Nile Thompson for their assistance in translating and interpreting Lushootseed (*xʷelšucid*) song texts.

*Appendix: Documented Versions of the Story
and Song of Dirty Face*

STORY AND RECORDED SONG FROM SAME RACONTEUR

1) Annie Daniels (Duwamish)—Leon Metcalf, collector. Unpublished story, including song—"Story of *spitsxʷp*" (in Lushootseed [Duwamish]); recorded May 1, 1954. Unpublished English translation of story by Vi Hilbert.

2) Lizzie Martin (Lummi)—Lushootseed Research, collector. From unpublished portion of "Sharing Legends at Upper Skagit" (video-recording); recorded March 25, 1985. Story about Snipe and his Southwind parents (English); song in Skagit(?).

3) Jerry Kanim (Snoqualmie)—Warren Snyder, collector. Published story text—"Snow Bird" (told in Lushootseed [Snoqualmie] and published with English translation) (Snyder 1968: 48–51); collected August 1955.

4) Henry Allen (Twana)—William Elmendorf, collector. Published story text—"Snowbird as South Wind" (told in English) (Elmendorf 1961: 104); collected 1939 or 1940. Unpublished song recording—"Snowbird's Song to his South Wind Uncles" (song text in Lushootseed); collected in 1946.

STORY AND RECORDED SONG FROM DIFFERENT RACONTEURS
BUT RELATED IN COLLECTION

1) Snuqualmi Charlie (Snoqualmie) and Jack Stillman (Snoqualmie)—Arthur C. Ballard, collector. Published story text—"The Man Who Would Not Wash His Face" as told by Snuqualmi Charlie (first of four versions of story collected by Ballard in original language between 1916 and 1929, published in English only) (Ballard 1929: 49).

2) Unpublished song recording—Arthur C. Ballard, collector. Unpublished song from "The Man Who Would Not Wash His Face," sung by Jack Stillman (Snoqualmie); recorded June 1932. It does not exactly match any of the four versions of the story collected by Ballard but is closest to that of Snuqualmi Charlie.

STORY IN PRINT FORM INCLUDING SONG TEXTS

1) Peter Heck (Upper Chehalis)—Thelma Adamson, collector (1926). Published story text in English titled "The Flood" (Adamson 1934: 1–2); includes song text—"Father-in-law, mother-in-law, Keep moving back from the river."

2) Mary Iley (part upper Cowlitz Taitnapam, mainly lower Cowlitz Coast Salish in tribal identification [Jacobs 1934–37: 125]);

Thelma Adamson, collector (1927). Published story text in English titled "The Flood" (Adamson 1934: 178); includes song texts (three song sections in story)—"Brothers-in-law, brothers-in-law / I'm going to wash my face, I'm going to wash my face" (two times); "Brothers-in-law, brothers-in-law / I'm going to wash my face / I'm dancing now"; "Brothers-in-law, brothers-in-law / I'm bathing now, I'm bathing now." The source of this published version appears to be an undated entry in Adamson's notes—"Thrush. Little Brown Bird" by Mary Iley (Miller 1999a: 55); the main difference is the use of both *Thrush* and *spicxʷ* in the notes but only *spicxʷ* in the published version.

3) Christine Smith (Green River)—Arthur C. Ballard, collector. Published story text in English titled "The Man Who Would Not Wash His Face" (second of four versions of story collected by Ballard in original language between 1916 and 1929, published in English only) (Ballard 1929: 50); includes song text—*bo'lə bo'lə sxʷə' otso'təbtcid / kya'kəkwiə ko'sib / sxʷo'lgwad xʷwə'.*

4) Joe Young (Puyallup)—Arthur C. Ballard, collector. Published story text in English titled "The Man Who Would Not Wash His Face" (fourth of four versions of story collected by Ballard in original language between 1916 and 1929, published in English only) (Ballard 1929: 50); includes song text—*syəlyəla'b əd kwi'akako'sib tci'cub tci'cub* ("Uncles, I am washing my face; rain in long drops, rain in long drops!").

5) Chief William Shelton (Tulalip)—collector? Published story text in English titled "Sparrow Washes His Face" (Hilbert 1996); story dated "1923" [?]; includes English song text—"Let the rain come down in torrents . . . for I have been told to wash my face!"

STORY ONLY (RECORDINGS OR PRINT FORM)

1) Emma Conrad (Sauk)—Thom Hess, collector (1963). Unpublished story on audiotape; story transcription by Toby Langen for Tulalip Tribes; no songs.

2) Ann Jack (Green River)—Arthur C. Ballard, collector. Published story text—"The Man Who Would Not Wash His Face" (third of four versions of story collected by Ballard in original language between 1916 and 1929, published in English only) (Ballard 1929: 50); no songs.

3) Joe Pete (Upper Chehalis)—Thelma Adamson, collector (1926). Published story fragment (Adamson 1934: 3); no songs.

4) Jonas Secena (Upper Chehalis)—Thelma Adamson, collector
(1926). Published story text—"The Flood" (Adamson 1934: 2–3);
no songs.

SONG ONLY (RECORDINGS)

1) Marion Davis (Upper Chehalis; mother from White River; Nis-
qually and Puyallup relations [Kinkade 1991: viii])—Thelma
Adamson, collector. No corresponding story by Marion Davis
in published volume. Unpublished song recording (from White
River; text in southern Lushootseed?); recorded in 1927. Published transcription by George Herzog (text phonetically transcribed by Franz Boas?) (Adamson 1934: 429).

2) Martha Lamont (Snohomish)—Thom Hess, collector. Unpublished song recording (Snohomish); recorded on August 4,
1966.

References

Adamson, Thelma. 1934. *Folk-Tales of the Coast Salish.* Memoirs of the American
Folk-lore Society 27. New York: American Folklore Society.

Amoss, Pamela T. 1978. *Coast Salish Spirit Dancing: The Survival of an Ancestral
Religion.* Seattle: University of Washington Press.

Ballard, Arthur C. 1929. "Mythology of Southern Puget Sound." *University of
Washington Publications in Anthropology* 3, no. 2: 31–150.

Bates, Dawn, Thom Hess, and Vi Hilbert. 1994. *Lushootseed Dictionary.* Seattle:
University of Washington Press.

Bierwert, Crisca, ed. 1996. *Lushootseed Texts: An Introduction to Puget Salish
Aesthetics.* Lincoln: University of Nebraska Press.

Elmendorf, William W. 1961. "Skokomish and Other Coast Salish Tales." 3 pts.
Research Studies of Washington State University 29, no. 1: 1–37; no. 2: 84–117;
no. 3: 119–50.

Farrer, Claire R. 1997. "Myth." In *Folklore: An Encyclopedia of Beliefs, Customs,
Tales, Music, and Art,* edited by Thomas A. Green, 575–81. Santa Barbara:
ABC-CLIO.

Frey, Rodney, and Dell Hymes. 1998. "Mythology." In *Plateau,* vol. 12 of *Handbook of North American Indians,* edited by Deward E. Walker, 584–99. Washington, D.C.: Smithsonian Institution Press.

Hilbert, Vi. 1996. *Haboo: Lushootseed Literature in English.* 1980. Reprint, Seattle: Lushootseed Press.

Hilbert, Vi, and Jay Miller, trans. 1995. *Aunt Susie Sampson Peter: The Wisdom
of a Skagit Elder.* Seattle: Lushootseed Press.

Jacobs, Melville. 1934–37. *Northwest Sahaptin Texts.* Columbia University Contributions to Anthropology 19. New York: Columbia University Press.

Kinkade, M. Dale. 1991. *Upper Chehalis Dictionary.* University of Montana
Language Laboratory, Occasional Papers in Linguistics 7. Missoula: University
of Montana.

Langen, Toby C. S., and Bonnie Barthold. 1991. "The Texts Are Compelling:

Introduction to This Issue." *SAIL (Studies in American Indian Literatures)*, ser. 2, 3, no. 1: 1–7.

Miller, Jay. 1999a. "Chehalis Area Traditions: A Summary of Thelma Adamson's 1927 Ethnographic Notes." *Northwest Anthropological Research Notes* 33: 1–72.

———. 1999b. *Lushootseed Culture and the Shamanic Odyssey: An Anchored Radiance*. Lincoln: University of Nebraska Press.

Ramsey, Jarold. 1999. *Reading the Fire: The Traditional Indian Literatures of America*. Rev. ed. Seattle: University of Washington Press.

Silver, Shirley, and Wick R. Miller, eds. 1997. *American Indian Languages: Cultural and Social Contexts*. Tucson: University of Arizona Press.

Snyder, Warren A. 1968. *Southern Puget Sound Salish: Texts, Place Names, and Dictionary*. Sacramento: Sacramento Anthropological Society.

Thompson, Laurence C., and M. Dale Kinkade. 1990. "Languages." In *Northwest Coast*, vol. 7 of *Handbook of North American Indians*, edited by Wayne P. Suttles, 30–51. Washington, D.C.: Smithsonian Institution Press.

Wiget, Andrew. 1985. *Native American Literature*. Boston: Twayne Publishers.

4 | Drum, Songs, Vibrations
Conversations with a
Passamaquoddy Traditional Singer

FRANZISKA VON ROSEN
(Introduction by Tara Browner)

The Passamaquoddy *(Peskotomuhkati)* and Maliseet *(Wolas-toqiyik)* are closely related but politically independent peoples who share very similar languages. They are historically part of the Wabanaki Alliance together with the Abenaki, Penobscot, and Mi'kmaq nations. These tribal nations straddle the national borders of the United States and Canada, in areas now called Maine and the Canadian Maritimes (New Brunswick and parts of Quebec). Prior to contact with Europeans, their traditional cultures revolved around fishing and farming during the summer and hunting in the winter months.

Wabanaki populations were decimated during the seventeenth and eighteenth centuries by smallpox and other diseases brought by European settlers, and in the late nineteenth and early twentieth centuries, children from these communities were taken to be educated in boarding schools. The resulting erosion of language skills and traditional culture is a direct consequence of children in these settings being discouraged from speaking in their native language.

Maggie Paul, who is interviewed in the article, is a prime mover in the ongoing revitalization of traditional singing in Maliseet and Passamaquoddy communities. The interview, in the form of a conversation, is conducted by her friend Franziska von Rosen, and is in a style known as "dialogic," which was first pioneered in ethnomusicology by Judith Vander in her groundbreaking work *Songprints: The Musical Experience of Five Shoshone Women* (1988). A significant difference in the interview styles, however, is that von Rosen does not interpret or analyze Paul's remarks, although she does guide the conversation to some extent.[1]

• • •

There was a time when the sound of the drum had ceased at St. Mary's Reserve, the home of members of the Maliseet Nation, in New Brunswick, Canada. The silence lasted for two generations. In 1980, the drum—"the heartbeat of the nation"—started beating. That sound "isn't going to get lost again," said Maggie Paul, the drum keeper for the community and a founding member of the Wabanoag Singers.

I met Maggie Paul and other members of the St. Mary's community for the first time in 1985 while doing research for the SPINC project.[2] Although I interviewed Maggie at that time, my real learning about her music happened more informally. Over the next ten years I had many opportunities to learn from her and other traditional musicians in the Maritimes. When I showed a personal interest, I was invited to participate in ceremonies. There were wonderful social occasions, like the "socials" in Maggie's house, when people got together informally to drum and chant, to share food and laughter and stories. As I got to know some of the songs, I was invited to sing and later to join them at the drum. For me, Maggie has become a special friend, a person I enjoy singing with, a woman I respect.

Over the years Maggie has helped me understand many aspects of the music that she and others on the reserve perform. Often, the way she talks about music is in stark contrast to the way that ethnomusicologists have traditionally tried to study it. For example, scholars are usually concerned with establishing boundaries or categories that classify musics, and tend to set up dichotomies such as: traditional-contemporary, authentic-inauthentic, ours-theirs, sacred-social. These categories reflect academic interests in issues of authenticity, ownership, function, and use. Other areas of research are related to gender roles and to the way people individually or socially "construct" their identities, and again scholars frequently think in terms of oppositions self-other, insider-outsider. Maggie's approach, on the other hand, was inclusive, and boundaries that concern Western academics represented no significant meanings for her. Getting the drum to sound again, finding songs and singing them for the Creator, making sure that the next generation has songs to sing—those are the issues and focus of her life.

When we were invited to contribute an article for this volume, Maggie and I decided we would just sit together and talk about music. I wanted to have the conversation reflect those areas that she considers important. At the same time I also wanted to make sure the reader would get enough contextual information, not just through me summarizing it, and thereby giving it a different status, but through our conversation. Stanley Paul, Maggie's husband, briefly joined in the conversation when we started talking about the loss of traditional music and language on the reserve. Stanley, who is Maliseet, was born and raised in St. Mary's. Maggie is Passamaquoddy and came to the reserve in 1961, at age fourteen.

I recorded the conversations over two days. In editing them I rearranged the order only to add clarity to the text. I also deleted redundancies. After completing a first draft, I sent a copy to Maggie for her to edit and to suggest a title. The final draft is a product of our collaborative efforts. Having read my comments about meeting her, Maggie added her own thoughts on our relationship: "Together [Franziska] and I make good music."

The Beginning

Franziska: Let's start at the beginning, Maggie. The drum had stopped beating. Nobody was singing the old songs on the reserve. What happened next?

Maggie: It was some time around the late '60s, about 1968 or '69. Well, Alma [Brooks] and I would visit each other, and we'd talk about what we would like for our kids and our grandchildren, what we would want them to remember, what we would want them to do. We'd talk every day, and we'd say, "We should do something." But we just kept talking and talking. Then one day we decided, we're going to do it. So we did. We started going down home to get some songs.

Franziska: Why did you have to go searching for songs to sing? Were there no songs at St. Mary's? Why did you go down home, down to Sipayik [Pleasant Point] in Maine? What about closer to home?

Maggie: Well, we couldn't find any here. Didn't know anybody who knew any songs. But I knew my cousin Deanna had already started thinking about songs ten years before we started. And we needed songs. We *had* to do something. At that time we knew one song, "Kwanute." That was the only one we knew how to sing. We sang that all over the place. Just that one song. This was maybe '73, '74. We got it from down home too because, you know, when I was a kid they always had those Indian Days. I remember Auntie Mary, Mary Moore, used to teach the kids to dance. As I grew up I remembered that song that they used to sing.

The very first songs we got from them were ones they had learned from the Mohawk people in Akwesasne. So we sang those. After that we picked up songs here and there. Someone would say, "Here,

I'll give you a song. You can sing this one." We had a hard time finding songs, but we kept on going. Tom [Paul]—we learned a lot of songs from him.[3] The songs that he sang, the pow-wow songs, those were the ones that we started singing. But there was one song that he said he got from an old spirit woman, that prayer song. I only sing the chant part. I do not know what he is saying in Mi'kmaq.

Franziska: A lot of the songs that Tom was singing were ones that he had picked up during his travels through western Canada and the United States in the 1970s. So were those the kinds of songs you were looking for? What were you and Alma looking for, Maggie?

Maggie: Didn't matter if it was our songs or anybody else's songs. As long as they were Indian songs, it didn't matter. To *us* it didn't matter. In those days nobody said you shouldn't sing this song or that song. Nobody said anything. I remember one time an elder who said to us, "You can sing forever. I don't want to hear anybody telling you not to sing because of the power that goes with the song. When you sing the song," he said, "everybody feels it." That's what he was saying, that elder.

If your singing makes somebody feel good, if you make somebody smile, that's good. Feel what is in your heart and go with that, sing that. That's what I think.

Why Had the Drum Stopped?

Franziska: Maggie, can you talk about why the old people stopped singing in St. Mary's?

Maggie: They had to . . .

Stanley: I think the last time they sang was in the '40s, '50s, down on the old reserve. They even had a longhouse then, remember? It was the same reserve but at a different location, and they just moved from there up to where it is now.

Franziska: So why had the people stopped singing?

Maggie: I think these old people, the ones that we call old people that are living on the reserve now, the ones that are alive now, they don't remember them. I think their grandparents did.

Franziska: If I think about what generation the songs got lost or left behind from what the Mi'kmaq elder Michael Francis told me, then it seems to have been Mike's grandfather's generation that were the last to really know the old songs. He only remembered bits of them.

Maggie: Yeah. What happened?

Franziska: The way Mike described it was that his father felt there was "no future in the songs and dances." "That's foolishness" is what Mike said his father told him.

Maggie: You hear that also with some of the elders talking about the language. What's the sense? They say we have to move on, go out there and be with the white people. We might as well not speak the language because it is not important to us anymore. Now that's devastating.

Stanley: Well, I think they didn't want us to go through the same thing they did, when they were going to school. So they stopped even teaching us the language. I mean, they got beatings for even talking it. So to save us from getting beatings, they didn't teach us the language and the songs.

Maggie: I think the last one to sing the songs was Louise Paul. Remember Louise?

Stanley: Yeah, because she even knew the deer dance. That was way back, a long time ago, when she was a young girl.

Maggie: Well, way back, the older people were made to feel, and were being told, that it's no use. We heard that they were forced not to sing their songs and not speak their language and to hide their drums and hide their pipes. When the missionaries came, the Catholics, they were saying our God was the devil.

Stanley: They were made to be afraid.

Maggie: Yeah, our grandparents were made to feel afraid. It would have to be because when these people came, our people must have believed them. But I just don't know how it all started.

Stanley: Well, the way my mother explained it was that they were trying to save us from getting beatings, especially when going to school. Then when they got older, they knew they had made a mistake in not teaching us the language and the songs, but it was too late, basically.

Maggie: When I was going to school—that was, well, I'm almost fifty now—I wanted to sing. I wanted to sing to the Creator. But the only songs I knew were the songs that were sung on the radio, those old holy, holy songs. Those were the songs that I sang. But I didn't know there was such a thing as Indian songs for a long time.

Franziska: Do you remember your mother or your grandmother ever singing songs?

Maggie: Just humming. They used to hum a lot. And I used to watch my grandmother lullabying her babies, her grandchildren. Just humming. It must have been something that just came to her, from the connection to the baby she was just holding. I do that myself when I hold Possesom, Autumn, or Dakota [Maggie's grandchildren]. The little ones *need* that lullaby, that humming song. It's not something you know beforehand. It becomes a tune when you are humming. My grandmother, I can still hear her, just like sweetgrass.

Sweetgrass is another sound. Oh, if I could hum that—oh, I know I could. My mother when she was braiding that, you would hear that sweetgrass music. Squeaky, but within that squeaky sound, that tone. The grass is hooked onto a wooden chair, and you hear that wood and the sweetgrass and that water, just like this [rubs her fingers together], and it's going fast, and you hear *that* sound [Maggie bursts into laughter], I would just put my head on that wood and my mother would be braiding away and I would fall asleep. And then when I woke up I would have this sweetgrass juice all over my face, all over my clothes [laughs]. But it felt so good, eh.

The Songs

Franziska: In your search for songs, Maggie, what were some of the ones that belong here to the Wabanaki Nations, and can you talk about them a bit?

Maggie: Well, "Kwanute" was the only song we had for a while. I remember one day I asked, "What is 'Kwanute,' Uncle Joe?"[4] He told me that *Kwan* means welcome and then *Kwanute* is a place of dance where they used to gather. It would be like a hall or outside somewhere, and they danced the "Kwanute" to welcome the other people that came.

Franziska: So does that mean that you would start with this song?

Maggie: Usually I like to start out with "Kwanute" or "Ekwanute." Or the upbeat version of "Kwanute"—I like to start out with that one, too.

Franziska: So "Kwanute" has many different versions?

Maggie: Many different ways, but it all means the same; it is all a place of welcome. Many different ways of singing it and many different ways of using it. Just like that song I heard Jerry Padilla singing on tape somewhere.[5] When I heard him sing that, I wanted to learn it right away. He said they used that a long time ago during the chief-making ceremonies. That was the inauguration song. It's beautiful.

Franziska: The "Kwanute" songs are also sung by the Mi'kmaq people. I have heard various groups performing that. I am thinking of Sarah Denny and the Eskasoni Singers from Eskasoni, Cape Breton, or George Paul of Red Bank, New Brunswick. George also talked about "Kwanute" as the welcoming song, and said it was meant to welcome all the people that would come to the traditional gatherings.[6]

What about the trading song that your group sings? Where did you get that one?

Maggie: I really don't know too much about that trading song. I only know that Carol Paul from Woodstock [New Brunswick] has that translated in Maliseet and English. I didn't even ask her, but she offered to share that song with us. That song belongs right there, in Woodstock, to the Maliseet people. People are singing it there.

We also sing the "Medicine Snake," but the only thing I know about that song is that when Jerry [Padilla] sang it I wanted to learn it [laughs]. I told him, "I *want* this song. I *need* it." It is so powerful because of the sound. The sound that's in that song, oh, it is powerful. There are some songs that you can sing and they are so beautiful and so mellow. But there are some songs that you *have* to sing; that's how I feel. I have to sing that song. Because of the sound that's in there—it's not that I have to have it; I have to put that in my voice, that sound. Because I recognize the sound, that's the only way that I can explain that. I don't know what the song means, but it has to do with snake medicine so I sing that song for the snakes. The ones that look after the medicine.

Franziska: That is what Tom [Paul] said about a snake song that he heard on the old Frank Speck tapes. After listening to it a few times he created his own version of the song because the quality of the old tapes was so poor that he could not make out the song entirely. But he also talked about a special sound in that song that he was drawn to. But you also have another medicine song that you sing.

Maggie: When we get all the people together I want to sing that song for them. Then I tell them, "This is a medicine song for everybody, so we can bring good medicine together here, with the people. After that I look around and think what songs I want to sing next for the people. Then sometimes I see kids, and I want to sing those peppy ones. They like the *fast* ones [laughs]. They just *want to dance.*

Franziska: There was also another dance that was called the Pine Needle Dance or *Tutuwas*?

Maggie: I don't know where that came from, but I heard that ages ago, down home. When Cosy Nicholas used to sing that for Indian Day. Then he sang that for the women. They say that is a woman's song and the women dance it.

What Is So Important about Having Songs?

Franziska: Maggie, you talk so passionately about *needing* songs. What is so important to you about having songs?

Maggie: You see, when I sing I'm in a spiritual place. The sound takes me there, just the sound. You see, not too long ago, at the house, I was just lying there on the bed, and all at once this flower appeared. That was the most beautiful flower that I have seen in my entire life. It looked like a star flower, and it was like velvet and the color of burgundy and cranberry mixed together. In the center of that flower there was a beam of light, and it was bright yellow. When I looked closely at that flower a shimmering voice came out, and this voice—it was a beautiful, beautiful sound. I know I can make that same sound, that high, crystal-clear, shimmering sound.

Franziska: Can you describe that tone?

Maggie: That, that electricity, or thunderbolt or lightning—yeah, that lightning when it goes all over, that's what it's like when you are singing. You can see that energy [Maggie is struggling to describe this sound and uses her hands to help her]. That's what music feels like to me.

Franziska: When it's right.

Maggie: Yes! [The energy has built up in the room, and both Maggie and I simultaneously release it and laugh.]

Franziska: What you are telling me, Maggie, reminds me of something that I heard an Ojibwe elder say about an "original sound" in the universe. He described it as a "shimmering sound" that went out in all directions. He related that sound to the gourd rattle, and described it as "the Creator's thoughts."[7]

Maggie: Really!

Franziska: It seems like now we are really talking about the heart of the music, and not about certain pieces of music.

Maggie: Yes! The heart of it. You know when you feel that music, the more you talk about it, the deeper you get, and the feeling you get is that energy, that force. [Silence.]

Making Her Own Songs

Franziska: Do you ever make your own songs, Maggie?

Maggie: I don't even know how to make a song [laughs]. I am always singing other people's songs, and I don't have one song, not even one song for myself. A lot of people are asking me to make songs, and I don't even know how. But this friend of mine, she said, "You don't have to worry, Maggie, 'cause the songs you are going to be singing, you don't even know where the words are going to come from, but they are going to come. You won't even have to make them up.

But I just want to sing something that the whole world could hear and get something from it, so that they could just say, "Hey, hold on a minute—this isn't what life is all about; *this* is what it's about." *We* should travel inward, instead of out here; travel with that sound. I mean, if we could put this whole world in a standstill and everybody would make that certain type of sound, oh, my God, we'd be [we both start laughing]—we'd be in orbit [laughter]!

Franziska: I don't know how long we could sustain that singing, that sound. I mean, after a while I'm seeing an image here of all of our voices together creating this energy and together keeping this ball or disc hovering in space [laughter].

Maggie: When you are singing, you are healing people. When you do that sound, you are vibrating that part of your body that is sick. The vibrating from the singing brings the good energy to that place and heals it. But you have to concentrate to do that type of healing, and a lot of people are not doing that. [Maggie's hands and feet are just exploding in all directions; the energy is moving her.]

Franziska: So what I am hearing you say is that it does not matter so much what song is being sung, but rather that of getting the sound right, the tone right, and the energy, and focusing everything on the task of healing.

Maggie: Yes!

Women Singing and Drumming

Franziska: Has the attitude to women singing around the drum changed in the last few years, Maggie? I remember we were down at Passamaquoddy and there was another Drum group, all men, and then there was your group and we were singing there. I remember that there was a certain tension in the air because of the women drumming. Has that changed, and how do you feel about it?

Maggie: It has changed somewhat. But a lot of the women weren't acknowledged; they weren't singing. So this is what I thought: "How come women aren't singing? How come they are not around the drum?" And then when we started singing, people started saying, "What are you doing around the drum?" Women are not supposed to be singing. Not supposed to be singing when everybody has got a voice? Why can't we sing? It feels good to sing. Why can't we share? And some places they just talked about us, but it did not stop me from singing. I wasn't going to stop singing. After a while we sang *with* the men. I love singing with the men, and that's hardly done anymore either. It says a lot when women sing. It says a lot when men sing. It says a lot when we all sing together. It's so *powerful.*

Franziska: So you don't limit yourself then?

Maggie: No, no, I don't. That's what that spirit told me when I went into the sweat lodge in Alberta. I was going to quit singing. I was going to quit everything. So that's the first thing that spirit said to me there. "I don't ever want to hear you say that again. You're going to quit telling your dreams," that's what he said. And he said the songs that you sing, it doesn't matter whether they belong to you. The songs of other nations, he said, sing them because—sometimes

we don't even know what we are singing—but he said, "It gets cor-
rected on the other side." They hear it on the other side, and they are
crying. They thought they would never ever hear the songs again.

The spirits are listening to you; the spirits hear and see and know
everything you do. They are always ready if you want to sing for
them; they are always ready. That's what the spirit told me, and
he even introduced himself—his name was Robin Blue Hair, and
he died nine years before I went to that lodge. He was one of the
elders there.

Franziska: How important then, as you were saying before, that everybody has a voice and that everybody has an opportunity to participate and to sing.

Maggie: Yes, because it's connecting with the earth energy, who we
are, where we came from. That tree knows everything. If they could
talk, they could tell you stories; they can talk. When we are out
there singing, you can see those trees dancing; they are so appre-
ciative. When you sing, you sing for Creation anyway. There are,
of course, some songs that I have to respect. Those I will not sing
just anywhere, no matter how much I may want to. That much I
know.

What's Happening on the Reserve Now?

Franziska: How do you feel now when you look back at the years of
struggle that you and Alma and some of the other people in the
community have gone through to bring the songs back?

Maggie: Fantastic, because that struggle was really worth it to bring
those songs back. No matter if somebody says, "Oh, you should not
be singing this song." I sing them anyway, because if we don't, if we
start listening to people, "Don't be singing the songs—don't be doing
this and that," might as well bury everything. There are still people
laughing at us. That's all right. They don't know. They just haven't
gone that far yet, to know. Even some of the people that come and
sing with us now say, "I used to laugh at these people, at the Wabanoag Singers, and here I am." Yeah, that is true. It took twenty
years down the road, but that's all right. If it will take forever, then
that's what it will take. But I know that they will be there.

Franziska: That must be a good feeling.

Maggie: Yeah. Because you know sometimes it takes a disaster, or
something happens for people to come together. And I know at
that time when they are feeling that way, it doesn't really matter
to them if anyone knows they are here singing with us. But other
times they don't want to. It's just that they are not used to it. They
haven't felt proud yet. Maybe some people still feel ashamed, feel

that they don't want to be Indian, because they don't know about themselves. So it's pretty hard for them.

That's why I allow these guys to drum at my place anytime, because they're struggling. They are between twenty and thirty, these guys that are drumming. I want them to keep drumming to keep singing. Sometimes you have to steer them straight. Knock their hats off once in a while [laughs]. But they are just learning. I know where they are at. I was there before, too. I'm still there once in a while. I'm still learning.

Sometimes they don't know how to do a song, and they ask me. Then I show them how I do it, and they take it from there. I don't tell them, "You should do it this way." I don't tell them that. I say, "This is how I do it, this is what I hear, but you can do whatever you want with it" [laughs]. They like that. Then they ask me to sing with them sometimes. But I'm just there. I make them coffee, or if I'm cooking something it is there. Sometimes we're not home, and they come in and sing, have coffee, pop, whatever is there.

Franziska: Have you ever thought of quitting again?

Maggie: Never again will I think that way, that I'll quit singing, because songs are going to live forever, and they are going to be passed down to all the kids. There are a lot of kids that want to learn now. Even three, four year olds are learning to sing all the songs that we sing.

Franziska: What about your grandchildren?

Maggie: Oh, Possesom knows the songs. He sings them. Sometimes when we get the drum out, then he'll get his drum out, the one Stanley made him. Then he'll get all the kids together. "This is a song I want to sing for you." So he will sing the songs. But they are so cute and so beautiful, it makes you feel so good when you see him, getting his drum out, putting tobacco on there, then talking with the Creator. You don't have to tell him anything or show him how to do it. He sees it. I don't have to say, "Come on, Possesom, this is what I want you to do." He already knows it and sees it. Yeah, that's what he does. Anybody that he knows needs help, he'll pray. Or if anybody needs a song, he will sing a song.

Franziska: And he has just turned seven [see fig. 4.1].

Maggie: Yeah, that sound, it's not going to get lost again. We have so much to learn about ourselves. If we listen to what our heart tells us, if we do things our way, we'll never go wrong. Listen to the drum, listen to our songs. *Da—ho.*

Figure 4.1. Margaret Paul and her grandson Possesom. Courtesy of Ann Billson.

Notes

1. For a previous conversation with Margaret Paul, see von Rosen and Paul 1990: 13–16.

2. SPINC is an acronym for "sound-producing instruments in Native communities." The work involved a comprehensive study of musical instruments in eastern woodlands communities, combining detailed description with social and cultural information. The research was done in association with Queen's University, Kingston, Canada, and funded by the Social Sciences and Humanities Research Council of Canada. The project was under the direction of Dr. Beverley Diamond (Cavanagh).

3. Tom Paul (Spotted Eagle) was the lead singer for the Birch Creek Singers of

Big Cove, New Brunswick. Tom, a Mi'kmaq from Eskasoni, Cape Breton, Nova Scotia, is honored by traditionalists in Atlantic Canada for having returned the drum tradition to the region.

4. Joseph Nicholas of Sipayik (Pleasant Point), Maine.

5. A Penobscot from Indian Island in Old Town, Maine.

6. See *Traditional Micmac Chants* (1991). On this recording George Paul sings various versions of "Kwanute," the welcoming song, a round dance, and another that he calls the "feast song."

7. See Diamond with Cronk and von Rosen 1994: 86.

References

Diamond, Beverley, with M. Sam Cronk and Franziska von Rosen. 1994. *Visions of Sound: Musical Instruments of First Nations Communities in Northeastern America*. Waterloo, Ontario: Wilfred Laurier University Press.

Vander, Judith. 1988. *Songprints: The Musical Experience of Five Shoshone Women*. Urbana: University of Illinois Press.

Von Rosen, Franziska, and Margaret Paul. 1990. In *The Sound of the Drum*. Compiled by M. Sam Cronk. Brantford, Ontario: Woodland Cultural Centre.

Selected Discography

Free Spirit: MicMac Mi'Kmaq Songs. Sunshine Records Ltd., Winnipeg, Manitoba, SSCT 4093.

Heart Beat 2: More Voices of First Nations Women. Smithsonian Folkways, CD SF-40455.

Traditional Micmac Chants. 1991. Eagle Call Singers (featuring George Paul). York Point Productions.

Traditional Voices from the Eastern Door. Featuring George Paul, James Augustine, and Donna Augustine. Produced and distributed by James Augustine, Big Cove, New Brunswick.

Selected Videography

River of Fire Festival: Celebration of Life. 1995. Produced by Pinegrove Productions. Distributed by V-tape, Toronto, and Pinegrove Productions, R.R. #1, Lanark, Ontario. VHS, color, 55.40 minutes.

Nuji-atukwet Mi'kmawa'j: Jipuktewik Sipu [Micmac Storyteller: River of Fire]. 1991. Produced and directed by Franziska von Rosen and Michael R. Francis. Distributed by Pinegrove Productions, R.R. #1, Lanark, Ontario. VHS, color, 35 minutes.

5 Identity, Retention, and Survival

Contexts for the Performance
of Native Choctaw Music

DAVID E. DRAPER

As the current revival of interest in American Indian music expands our knowledge about expressive behavior in contemporary Native American societies, music is being recognized by more and more researchers as a viable part of tribal cultures. Because of this increase in scholarly attention, brought about in many cases by the recent social and economic progress of indigenous groups, we are gaining new information about aesthetics, ideology, and symbolic behavior, among other possibilities. With this expansion of existing knowledge base, we may also expect a reexamination of previous research. Thus, we have an opportunity to reconsider and improve the quality of the material currently available, both to tribal members and to those outside of Indian communities. This chapter will aid the latter category, because although the music of the Mississippi Choctaw has been studied in the past, some of the information presented has been problematic in nature due to publication restrictions.[1]

Approximately nine thousand Choctaw still reside in Mississippi. About one thousand individuals remained in the original territory at the time of the "Trail of Tears," and it is from this group that the present population is descended. Choctaw speakers currently reside in seven communities in the vicinity of Philadelphia, Mississippi. Some individuals live on reservation land; others do not.

The changing economic pattern in Mississippi (and the South in general) over the past few decades has effected changes for the Choctaw. Particularly on an economic level, these people exhibit a high level of acculturation. Yet in other spheres of their lives, they retain a distinctive Choctaw identity. Prominent in this retention of identity is the maintenance of Native ideological and symbolic systems. Choctaw is still the first language of many in this population, and although men are forced to learn English in order to compete economically, many older women, especially in conservative communities, still refuse to speak English. The institution of the Native shaman still has meaning as a viable part of this culture, and it is the shaman's role to verbalize aspects of the ideology for Choctaw speakers. Contributing to the retention of a unique identity is their aboriginal musical system, much of which probably survives from the precontact era. As will be examined below, this repertory is highly symbolic and intimately linked with the ideological system of the Choctaw.

The degree of acculturation or assimilation for the Mississippi Choctaw remains a complex issue, with the seven communities forming a continuum from the conservative or traditional to the acculturated. Christian missionaries entered Choctaw country in 1819, and the continuing presence of such individuals has been a critical factor in the degree of acculturation exhibited. For traditional anthropological descriptions, the reader is referred to the publications of John R. Swanton (1911; 1931) and David Bushnell (1909). A more contemporary perspective may be found in John Peterson (1970).

An Overview of Choctaw Music

At present the musical system of the Mississippi Choctaw includes both indigenous and acculturated musical forms.[2] Although I will focus on specific elements of the musical repertory from the precontact period, it seems advisable to provide an overview of all existing categories of musical performance, allowing the reader to then place the subsequent discussion within the larger framework of contemporary Choctaw society.

The ethnographic literature on the Choctaw from the early postcontact years is not as complete as that available for some tribes. Thus, our knowledge of ritual and ceremonial life is extremely limited. We do not know, for example, if the Choctaw had attained a "state religion," as was reported for the neighboring Natchez Tribe. If such a level of cultural complexity were achieved, complete with priests and associated characteristics, we have no understanding of how the institution of the Native shaman would have interlocked with such communal ritual structures in aboriginal Choctaw life.

The only precontact ritual of which we have retained some knowledge is the stickball game. The ideological, political, and economic functions of this occasion are, in large part, described in the ethnographic literature mentioned above (and can be seen in 1830 period paintings by George Catlin). Extant examples of the associated musical repertory are rare; however, I was fortunate in obtaining a recording of one ball-game song from a Native shaman in 1969, shortly before his death. Another piece, the *Hogalillie, ho!* (reportedly sung by the players before the game), was recorded by an elderly song leader. Frances Densmore (1943) includes two transcriptions of flute songs performed by the shaman that are no longer remembered. These examples constitute the extant knowledge of ball-game music, which presumably was a rich repertory. As is illustrated by comparable examples cross-culturally, when the occasion for performance of music ceases to exist, the related musical repertory also disappears.

A relatively intact repertory of Native music referred to as *hitla tuluwa* (dance songs) has survived to the present day.[3] This music is performed outdoors, almost exclusively by groups of Choctaw speakers, and represents what does remain of the aboriginal ceremonial complex of the Mississippi Choctaw. Since these dance songs form the basis of the present chapter, the occasions for their performance will be discussed in detail.

Apart from the *hitla tuluwa* category, very few examples of the Native music have survived. I have been fortunate in collecting several miscellaneous songs, including a "lazy song," a lullaby, and a drinking song (based on the indigenous corn beer). A personal song sung by the ballplayers before going to the ball field was recorded, although it is unclear whether this example should be considered part of the "ritual" category of Native music.

The Beginnings of Acculturation: Abba isht tuluwa

With Christian missionaries having entered Choctaw territory shortly after the turn of the nineteenth century, a repertory of Christian hymns, the *Abba isht tuluwa* (God songs), emerged soon thereafter. Hymnbooks, containing only the texts of these hymns, were published as early as 1827, and continue to be printed and used in the Protestant Choctaw churches. The texts of 160 hymns appear in the current edition of this hymnal. Thirty melodies, used interchangeably with the various texts, have been collected and transcribed. Two of these examples have identifiable models: "In the Sweet Bye and Bye" and "Amazing Grace." An unpublished dissertation suggests that other examples may have preexisting melodic models (Stevenson 1976).

These hymns are similar in many respects to the *hitla tuluwa* repertory. Performances of the hymns have traditionally been led by a male song leader, following the practice exhibited in the aboriginal music. Melodic outlines are based on the whole-tone scale and are primarily pentatonic, with no influence of harmony in the monophonic melodic out-line that is sung unaccompanied. Women double the male vocal part an octave higher, as in the *hitla tuluwa* repertory. Texts are set exclusively in the Choctaw language, and those that have been translated suggest that the texts, at least, were original contributions of the Choctaw and the missionaries. These pieces continue to be performed in the Baptist and Methodist churches in the seven communities. Their popularity appears to be waning, but this may be a reflection of the non-Indian missionaries who currently reside there.

Oboha hitla

The *oboha hitla* (inside dances) currently represent the most popular of the acculturated musical forms. Since this repertory is classified in the *hitla,* or dance, category, it is distinguished from the aboriginal dances by being designated as "inside" songs, that is, songs to be performed indoors, in contrast to the *hitla tuluwa.* They are performed at weekend nights, preferably Saturday evening, in the home of the Choctaw family sponsoring the dance. Since the fiddle and guitar players are paid, they may be regarded as professional musicians.

This purely instrumental repertory for fiddle and guitar contains versions of the fiddle repertory that have diffused from Appalachia and other regions. Titles include "Sally Gooden," "Orange Blossom Special," and "Old Joe Clark," to cite a few of the more familiar pieces. Although some pieces do not have specific titles, no research has been initiated on whether they are original compositions of Choctaw speakers. Probably, the titles of the borrowed songs have simple been forgotten.

Other Acculturated Musical Forms

Radio and television have expanded the listening genres for the Choctaw. In the vicinity of Philadelphia, Mississippi, country-and-western musical styles predominate in public broadcasting programs. This influence is being felt by the Choctaw and is evidenced by the recent formation of similar electrically amplified bands. Since 1969 there seems to have been at least one active band in existence, although the personnel has changed periodically. A few Choctaw occasionally participate in the established white country-and-western ensembles that practice and perform in the area.

In the Protestant churches on the reservation, the denominational hymnals, Broadman Hymnal, and Methodist Hymnal are now used extensively in the church services. Most often accompanied by piano or pump organ, the melody of the hymn is sung monophonically. "Hymn sings" are featured in the Protestant churches on Sunday afternoons when a fifth Sunday occurs in the course of a month (for further discussion of musical acculturation, see Draper 1971, 1975).

The Contemporary *hitla tuluwa* Repertory

The Mississippi Choctaw refer to the *hitla tuluwa* as "social dances." The term *social* should be understood to mean "communal," as opposed to "individual," and it would be inappropriate to convey the sense of secular in the western European parlance to this repertory of music in this context. The Mississippi Choctaw do not divide reality into sacred and secular dichotomies, underscoring a philosophy that is reflected in other North American Indian tribes. Existing evidence tends to support the thesis that these songs represent what remains of the ritual music of the Choctaw.

The songs I have analyzed illustrate how the *hitla tuluwa* formed the core of the communal ceremonial repertory prior to contact, and a growing literature on the subject suggests that ritual (or religious) music is highly retentive cross-culturally. Animal dances figure prominently in this musical category, and my field experiences suggest that animal symbols played a critical role in the precontact aboriginal ideology, including ritual, curing, and cosmology. Further, the Choctaw drum is closely associated with these pieces, with the drum reported to have occupied a role of importance in critical ceremonial observances, including the stickball game. Statements made by older specialists indicate that the drum was traditionally associated with shamanistic activities, and it still serves the important function of maintaining continuity in the performances of dance songs.

A large number of *hitla tuluwa* songs are remembered by older singers. The performance of these pieces, however, no longer plays a major role in Choctaw life, although demonstrations are performed for the public at the annual Choctaw fair each summer. Occasions for the performance of this music, however, do continue to exist in the more conservative Choctaw communities. Performances seem to be focused around the homes of the respected singers and appear to be impromptu gatherings of individuals rather than planned events.

When my field research on this music was initiated in 1969, only a few older individuals (Native speakers) remembered and were able to perform the dance songs; the repertory was in danger of becoming extinct. But by the early 1970s, the *hitla tuluwa* had been introduced into the curriculum of the Choctaw schools, at both elementary and secondary levels. With the renewed interest in preserving Choctaw identity on the reservation, this repertory is undergoing a revitalization, and is regularly performed by groups in both Mississippi and Oklahoma (Levine 1993).

Instruments and Their Role in Performance

The instruments used to accompany performance of the *hitla tuluwa* are striking sticks known as *etiboli*. Approximately half of the existing *hitla tuluwa* repertory employs this instrumental support. Striking sticks appear only with the song leader, who normally does not participate in the dancing. Undoubtedly, the primary reason that only one set of striking sticks has been observed is that the dance formations rarely free the hands for manipulating instruments.

Etiboli are usually constructed from hickory trees, which are reported to offer the "ideal" sound. The length of the sticks varies, although the majority of examples were approximately eighteen inches long. For practice sessions or recording sessions held for me, informants used whatever wooden materials were available.

Drums are intimately linked with the *hitla tuluwa* repertory, but they do not function in the role of accompaniment. The drum is played between songs within the song cycle. That is, the drummer begins to play at the termination of a piece and continues until the song leader initiates a new song. Only one rhythmic pattern is exhibited in this context, a repeating single-eighth-note, double-sixteenth-note ostinato. The drum *(ha the pa chitto)* is preferably constructed from black-gum wood, although cyprus, hard pine, poplar, and sweet gum may be used. Drum makers search for a tree trunk that is already hollow and scrape the interior to achieve the desired thickness, approximately one-fourth to one-half inch. The height of the drum depends on the diameter of the tree trunk and its thickness. Drums that I measured were about ten inches high and twelve inches in diameter. The drum head *(aspumon)* is preferably goatskin, although sheep hides are also employed. The skin is attached to the drum by a hickory rim, approximately one-half inch in width. The two sticks used as beaters *(ishit boli)* are constructed from hickory.

In current public performances of the *hitla tuluwa*, the dancers wear small metal jingle bells that are purchased locally. A number of these bells are attached in a cluster through a belt loop on the left side of the body. It is unclear whether the jingle bells are a new addition or a substitution for an earlier Native idiophone. The bells appear to have been used within the time span covered by the memory of present informants; older informants do not recall any item preceding the bells. It is likely, however, that jingle bells offer a new representation of an older sound. Given the prominence of idiophonic instruments among other tribes in

North America, including the southeastern cultural area, one may assume that originally a similar sound was produced by natural instruments—for instance, turtle shell, horn, or hoof rattles. Since jingle bells are not used in the music practice sessions, or in sessions arranged for recording purposes, I question, however, whether they are to be considered part of the musical system or regarded simply as an aspect of costuming.

Contexts for Musical Performance

In the precontact period, performances of the *hitla tuluwa* appear to have been held only at night and to have continued until dawn. The frequency of these occasions is not reported in the early literature on the Choctaw. Today, these performances are led exclusively by male song leaders, referred to as *entuluwa*. Both men and women participate in the dancing group, and the performers may alternate throughout the evening. The only restrictions for participants concern some songs in which relatives, that is, clan members, of the opposite sex are not permitted to perform.

There remains a large repertory of songs in the *hitla tuluwa* category that presumably dates from precontact times. The following list contains the titles of pieces I recorded:

Jump Dance	Turtle Dance
Walk Dance	Coon Dance
Changing Partners Dance	Bird Dance
Wedding Dance	Snake Dance
Drunk Dance	Turkey Dance
War Dance	Tick Dance
Muskogie Dance	Duck Dance
Falama (Backward and Forward)	Quail Dance
Beaver Dance	Bear Dance
	Gnat Dance

Certain titles, for example—Jump Dance, Walk Dance, Drunk Dance, and War Dance—serve as cover terms for a large number of specific pieces. To cite one example, fifteen different Walk Dances were collected. At present, each animal dance is represented only by one specific song. The pieces currently retained in the repertory basically consist of strophes. This form may indeed be a simplification or reduction of earlier versions of these pieces. The leader-chorus, or call-and-response, style is typical of this repertory, with the women's chorus part doubling the men's vocal line at the octave, thus producing a monophonic texture.

My research on the Choctaw *hitla tuluwa* has provided additional information about the structure of the musical occasion for the performance of this repertory, with several hypotheses concerning the nature of this musical event. I was fortunate in finding an elderly singer whose father, many decades ago, served as a song leader for the Bogue Chitto community. My consultant asserts that the occasions for performing *hitla tuluwa* were always begun with the singing of a special song, called the *amona tuluwa* (found in the section on musical analysis).

In his monograph on the Choctaw of Bayou Lacombe, David Bushnell states that this group has "one dance ceremony, which is in reality a series of seven distinct dances, performed in rotation and always in the same order" (1909: 20). This series is cited as follows:

1. *Nanena hitkla* (Man dance)
2. *Shatene hitkla* (Tick dance)
3. *Kwishco hitkla* (Drunken-man dance)
4. *Tinsanale hitkla*
5. *Fuchuse hitkla* (Duck dance)
6. *Hitkla Falama* (Dance Go-and-come)
7. *Siente hitkla* (Snake dance)

There is no *nanena,* or "man," dance currently remembered by Choctaw singers. The accompanying description of the dance movements in Bushnell's article corresponds with that of the current *tolobli hitla,* or Jump Dance.[4]

Given the large number of *hitla tuluwa* retained in this category, I propose that Bushnell's report is incorrect, stemming from either lack of knowledge on the part of his consultants or the limited time he spent with the Bayou Lacombe Choctaw. Present specialists do assert that the *hitla tuluwa* are to be performed in cycles of seven songs. Consequently, since my initial field research on Choctaw music, I have attempted to determine the sequential ordering within the cycle. Older specialists have provided conflicting reports. One characteristic feature of the listings obtained was the appearance of the Jump Dance *(tolobli hitla)* as the initial song: thereafter, the order invariably changed. I have therefore concluded that the Jump Dance was a marker, or an indicator of significance, signaling the beginning of the cycle. This is reinforced by its position as the initial dance in Bushnell's ordering.

There appears to be additional evidence in support of this theory. The Jump Dance is the only dance, aside from some versions of the War Dance, in which only men sing. The absence of the women's part, then, would make the appearance of this song within the cycle a noteworthy occurrence. Exclusive of the Jump Dance, it is likely that the internal ordering of songs within the cycle was arbitrary and left to the discretion of the song leader. Frances Densmore (1943) provides no additional information; she cites Bushnell's description, yet apparently makes no effort to expand the available information.[5]

Musical Examples:
The Comparative Analysis of Six Songs

In the following section, both the *amona tuluwa* ("first" song) and the available versions of the Jump Dance will be discussed. This section is not intended to provide an exhaustive analysis; rather, what appear to be the salient, unique features will be explored. Note that when the chorus part is not represented in the transcriptions, I have inserted the associated vocables in the leader's text and placed them in parentheses, thus providing continuity between the discrete parts.

"First" Song: Amona tuluwa

The *amona tuluwa* differs from the other *hitla tuluwa* transcribed and analyzed in that there is no recurrent phrase pattern indicating a response from the singing group. One would therefore conclude that this opening song for the musical occasion was sung exclusively by the song leader *(entuluwa)*. The term *amona* means "first," indicating that this piece precedes the performance of the song cycles.

One of the significant features of the *amona tuluwa* is the obvious formal division into sections. This is marked by the repeated expression "yo yo!" as illustrated in the accompanying transcription (musical example 5.1). This division, rarely found in other examples, is underscored by the complementary distribution of vocables. The phoneme /æ/, which is quite prominent in the initial section, does not appear in the second section.

The marker for the end of the piece, "we! ya!" is one of a limited number of ending patterns in this repertory. "Yo! Yo!" never appears in the final position, thus forming complementary sets of markers for the *hitla tuluwa.* A unique feature of this piece is the tessitura of the vocal part. Covering an octave plus a fourth, it exhibits the widest range of any of the *hitla tuluwa* examples. The pitches of this piece reflect a minor modal outline, with G natural as the pitch center, and a heavy emphasis on this one tone, with some extended, sustained singing. In the second section, all phrases terminate on this pitch.

In the second section there is an obvious formal pattern: the phrases that appear in brackets are almost exact repetitions, whereas the phrases preceding such segments do not correspond to each other. These three subdivisions form a major portion of the second section. A concluding statement repeats some of the preceding phrases, yet without the requisite pattern.

Musical example 5.1. *Amona tuluwa.* Transcribed by David E. Draper.

Rhythmic patterns also serve to distinguish the two sections of this piece. The initial section is nonmetrical; after the section markers, the song continues with a purely metrical pattern. The seemingly triple meter is interesting because the Choctaw cultural numbers are four and seven. However, this metrical pattern would distinguish the *amona tuluwa* from the predominantly duple meter of the dance songs.

Jump Dance I

All dance songs are open-ended; they are repeated until terminated by the song leader. Thus, the ending signal occurs at the discretion of the song leader. In dances featuring a circle formation, the song is repeated until the dancers, usually a variable number of individuals, complete the circle. In the Jump Dances, circle formations do not occur, and therefore the length of the song is entirely dependent on the leader.[6] The transcriptions I appended to this paper were recorded out of context; therefore, I have taken the liberty of including the chorus part as it would appear in a performance context.

Jump Dance I contains repetition on two different levels. First, there is the obvious repetition of phrases, as if the leader were pairing the phrases in his part. That is, the immediate repetition of a phrase in the leader's part appears to be a model from which the piece is generated. Second, there is a repetition of sections, or the appearance of repetition, with some minor interpolated variations. These sections are indicated by brackets over the musical staff. The second bracketed section appears to be the model from which the other sections derive. Whether, in the past, the sections were to be repeated precisely is speculative. If indeed these songs were bound to a ritual context, one might expect a more rigid internal ordering of phrases.

The pitch system in the Jump Dances varies, if measured by scientific instruments sensitive to minute variations in frequency. This lack of stability may be attributable to the age of the leader, since he is an elderly singer. At present, information on the remainder of the repertory is insufficient to form pertinent conclusions. The melodic outline is built around the minor triad (E-G-B), although Jump Dance I is not exclusively anhemitonic (without half-steps), as might be anticipated. The whole-tone pattern is broken only at the beginning of phrases sung by the leader, thus producing a more "ornamental" effect.

Musical phrases are defined by both an up-glide and aspiration. These I shall refer to as "markers" or "indicators of significance" on the level of /phrase/. Both markers are found in the leader and chorus parts. The final marker on the level of /piece/ is "ya ho! yo!" which is the most common example in the category of Jump Dances and frequently observed in other pieces of the repertory.

This song is the only Jump Dance in which one rhythmic pattern
is maintained throughout in both leader and chorus phrases. Musical
examples 5.2 and 5.6 are the only Jump Dances that are metrical in the
western European sense.

The syllabic pattern of the vocables is significant because leader and
chorus have four-syllable phrases:

yo   ha   le   na
we   hi   yo   we

The vowel pattern is important in that the leader's part features mid
and high vowels; the chorus response exhibits mid and low vowels. The
contrast in vowel sounds is a notable organizing factor for this piece,
and it may be found in other examples of the *hitla tuluwa.* The number
four is an important cultural gestalt for the Choctaw, as well as for most
other North American Indian tribes.

Jump Dance II

On a formal level, Jump Dance II is organized by the appearance
of one musical phrase that recurs throughout the leader's part. This
phrase, noted in brackets over the musical staff in the accompanying
transcription, serves as a type of refrain for the piece, and it appears as
the opening and closing phrase sung by the leader (see musical example
5.3). Internally, the appearance of this refrain phrase is characterized by
its immediate repetition. The final statement is not repeated, which
reflects a pattern observed in the first Jump Dance.

Related to this refrain pattern is the appearance of an intermediary
phrase indicated by the letter *A* in the transcription. It is questionable
whether this phrase is to be included as part of the refrain concept. Since
the concept of paired phrases appears in other Jump Dances, this may
indeed be the overriding pattern in the present example. The problem is
complicated by the repetition of these refrain phrases. What is troublesome is that without repetitions, the refrain-A-refrain pattern forms a
total of three phrases, a number inconsistent with Choctaw ideology; the
pattern formed with repetitions (refrain-refrain-A-refrain-refrain) would
also be inconsistent with traditional Choctaw worldviews. Between appearances of these refrain phrases are variable numbers of additional
phrases in the leader's part. Hence, there is no overall formal pattern
that is consistent.

The response phrases of this example are distinctive for the Jump
Dance. There is a change in melodic pitches, although the vocables

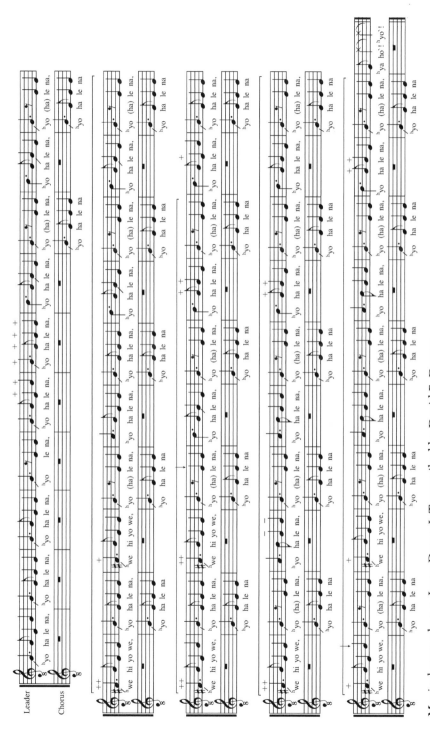

Musical example 5.2. Jump Dance I. Transcribed by David E. Draper.

Musical example 5.3. Jump Dance II. Transcribed by David E. Draper.

remain unaltered. This new melodic outline appears after the fourth solo phrase in the transcription. The occurrence of these changes is patterned: they appear immediately following the refrain-A-refrain section. Yet the solo phrases immediately preceding the changes are not identical. Such change must ultimately be effected by listening to the leader.

The indicators of significance defining the phrase in the response part include aspiration on both the initial pitch/vocable and the final pitch/vocable; this pattern is retained in the solo phrases with few exceptions. Textually, this dance song is reminiscent of the *amona tuluwa*, with the appearance of the phoneme /æ/ at the beginning of the piece. This phoneme occurs in the first three leader-chorus phrases and then ceases to appear. Thus, in both pieces it serves as an introductory pattern.

The leader, especially in refrain phrases, appears to take the chorus response as a model, which he extends to twice its length and manipulates both melodically and rhythmically. It is interesting that the leader's phrases derive textually from the syllabic pattern of the chorus. For example:

Musical example 5.3. Continued.

leader:	hi	yo	hi	yo	hi	ya	ha
chorus:	hi					ya	ha

The melodic outline is anhemitonic, with G natural serving as the pitch center. This tone is prominent in the response. The solo phrases terminate either on G natural or a third below, E natural.

A certain rhythmic flow is achieved in the longer solo phrases by manipulating the rhythmic structure. The syncopation observed occurs only internally, within the phrase; rhythmic stability marks the beginning and ending of the phrase.

Jump Dance III

The formal organization of the leader's part in Jump Dance III features a set of paired (repeated) phrases, which recur throughout the piece (see musical example 5.4). These are the first two phrases of the leader in the accompanying transcription, with the following vocable pattern: "o he ya yo he." Statements of this "refrain" set are separated by either one or

Musical example 5.4. Jump Dance III. Transcribed by David E. Draper.

two differing phrases. These interpolated phrases follow two basic melodic outlines, yet none is identical in pitch outline or textual underlay. The most important feature of the interpolated phrases is the change in syllabic pattern. The refrain vocables "o he ya yo he" become "wa [he/hi] o yo we." Another interesting linguistic feature is the phoneme /æ/, which the leader sings in the first two chorus responses. Thereafter, the phoneme changes to /a/.

Both up-glides and aspiration serve as phrase markers for the response phrases. The solo phrases contrast with other examples in the category of Jump Dances in that aspirations and up-glides are not used as indicators at the beginning of the phrase. Since the leader invariably overlaps with the initial response pitch, the up-glide and aspiration that operate as beginning markers for the chorus also serve as final phrase markers for the leader's phrases. The ending pattern, "ya ho! yo!" is the most frequently used signal for the repertory.

The pitch outline exhibits a whole-tone system, with no additional tones. The pitch center and ending tone are F natural. In rhythmic structure, both the leader and the chorus parts form a pattern of seven beats. The overlapping of phrases in the solo line produces an unbroken rhythmic flow.

Jump Dance IV

The form of Jump Dance IV is more highly organized than that observed in previous examples (see musical example 5.5). There are only four differing phrases sung by the leader, and these four are used interchangeably.

The solo part may be illustrated as follows:

A	B	A	B	C	D	B	C	D
	B	A	B	B	C	B		

What is of interest is the apparent grouping of three phrases. Given the general pattern of repeating or pairing phrases in the repertory, the initial pattern, established with the AB AB phrases, may continue with a cognitive grouping of two phrases on the part of the singer. Unfortunately, we do not have a recording of this song made in context, the length of which might determine the form precisely. Specialists are reluctant to verbalize about such matters.

The call-and-response pattern is not overlapping, as in previous examples. The lead singer breathes at the termination of his phrases, before joining with the choral response. These two adjacent phrases then become a discrete unit, producing distinct subsections within the piece. Both

Musical example 5.5. Jump Dance IV. Transcribed by David E. Draper.

leader and chorus parts are of equal length, the equivalent of six beats in Western terms. This rhythm is broken by the leader's C phrases, which contain four beats and produce a heterometric pattern.

The phrase marker in this piece is the heavy aspiration indicating the beginning of a phrase; this occurs for both solo and response parts. However, this indicator of the phrase occurs twice in each of the parts. The heavily stressed pitch at the beginning of the vocable pattern "he ya" supports this view, and creates an additional phrase. Becoming a marker itself, the musical phrase "he ya" designates the completion of the leader's part as well as the chorus part. Glottal stops terminate the solo phrases, thus forming a complex of features indicating the phrase unit.

The pitch outline is predominantly a whole-tone system; the pitch center is G natural, with all phrases terminating on this pitch. The C phrases in the solo part contain the half-step below G natural, and are the only deviations from the anhemitonic mode. There is an interesting pattern in the distribution of pitches: the chorus utilizes the principal tone and a fourth below; the leader sings mainly pitches above the pitch center. Both parts emphasize the pitch center, yet there is an obvious complementary distribution of the remaining tones utilized.

Jump Dance V: First Version

Jump Dance V has two different versions; they are cognitively recognized as being variants of the same song. The subsequent example is designated the "second version."

There is a symmetrical balance between the leader and chorus parts in the first version (see musical example 5.6). Both comprise four beats in rhythmic duration. Again, the discrete parts do not overlap, yet the phrases are sufficiently short that the leader needs only to take a breath at the termination of his phrase. This parallelism continues with the repetition of the response vocable pattern in the leader's text.

The pitch system is basically a whole-tone outline featuring the triad D–F sharp–A. A hint of major tonality appears in the fourth solo phrase and recurs in the eighth phrase, which suggests that this version may be of later origin than the succeeding one, and may show an influence of Western tonality. Since there is no formal ending pattern in the recording, it is assumed that the pitch center is D natural.

The formal organization of the leader's phrases may be clearly diagrammed:

A		A	B	C	D	A	A	C	B
		A	A	A	B'	B'	A		

The A phrase serves as a type of refrain, given its immediate repetition.

Musical example 5.6. Jump Dance V (first version). Transcribed by David E. Draper.

Up-glides invariably mark the beginning of the choral phrases, and often function in this manner for the leader. Aspiration is used concomitantly with the up-glides to designate the beginning of the phrase in both parts. The parallel use of the initial vocable "yo" might also be considered an indicator.

There is little rhythmic variety in this piece, which may be described as isometric. Both pitches and vocables appear on the beats. This rhythmic approach places this variant in sharp contrast to the second version.

Jump Dance V: Second Version

A number of factors suggest that the second version of Jump Dance V dates from an earlier period than the song described above. This example follows the whole-tone pitch outline exclusively, like the remainder of the repertory (see musical example 5.7). The rhythmic complexity, featuring what can be defined as syncopated, offbeat phrasing of accents, is more common to the *hitla tuluwa* songs. The extension, melodically and textually, of the choral pattern by the leader is also typical. Since the first version simply appears to be an abbreviated rendition of this song, I conclude that the present song is older.

Musical example 5.7. Jump Dance V (second version). Transcribed by
David E. Draper.

On a formal level, there is no consistent pattern in the solo phrases.
What is consistent is the ending phrase in the leader's part: "hi ya" always
appears on the same pitch, coinciding with the initial pitch of the following
choral response. The phrase markers remain the same, as discussed in the
preceding version.

The leader extends response phrases both textually and musically,
as observed in previous examples. Comparison of the vocable patterns
may be illustrated:

leader:	hi	yo	hi	yo	hi	yo	bi	hi	ya
[or]									
		hi	yo	hi	yo	bi	hi	ya	
chorus:			yo	bi	he	ya			

In rhythmic duration the solo phrases may be extended from four beats
to either six or eight beats, producing a heterometric (different meter)
pattern.

Thus, the parallelism between leader and chorus parts in the preceding song is not found in this piece, and the solo parts contain two phrases. The stress, aspiration, and up-glide at the beginning of the leader's "hi ya" imply that it is a distinct phrase.

Conclusion

In the preceding section, it is clear that the *amona tuluwa* and Jump Dance represent two different musical styles, or categories of style. The leader-chorus pattern is the most prominent distinguishing feature, although the lack of metrical orientation in the *amona tuluwa* is indeed a critical factor separating it from the remainder of the repertory. This factor tends to support my consultant's contention that the latter song was used as a marker for the musical occasion. As such, this information provides an important contribution to our knowledge of the structure of the occasion.

Some summary statements deriving from a comparison of the five individual Jump Dances would appear to be in order. The following eight points provide an overview of the significant features of this category:

1. No consistent pattern is observed to determine whether overlapping occurs between leader and chorus phrases.
2. The predominant orientation in the solo phrases provides for an "extension," or elongation, of the response phrases. This normally involves doubling the length of the response phrases.
3. Choral responses never extend beyond the interval of a fifth, with a wider tessitura observed in the solo phrases; the leader often employs the range of an octave.
4. The whole-tone, or anhemitonic, pitch outline is emphasized. Deviations from this pattern are primarily incidental tones. The resulting modal systems are both major and minor, according to the Western notion of tonality.
5. Chorus phrases terminate on the pitch center, yet the solo part is not restricted to ending with this pitch.
6. Phrase markers are consistent in these dances and include either up-glides, aspiration, dynamic stress, glottal stops, or a combination of these features.
7. There are a limited number of final markers on the level of / piece/, and they are consistent with the remainder of the repertory.
8. In rhythmic structure, the responses tend to be metrically patterned. Considerably more freedom is exhibited in the solo phrases, characterized by syncopation or offbeat phrasing of

melodic accents. The chorus, then, maintains a stable rhythmic foundation for the dancers; the leader is allowed the freedom of rhythmic manipulation. When the leader's phrases exhibit deviations from the metrical pattern, these invariably occur *internally*, within the phrase. Musical examples 5.2 and 5.6 are isometric in rhythmic organization; the remaining examples are heterometric.

In comparing linguistic components, the length of the syllabic form in leader phrases contains four, five, seven, or nine units; the choral part contains three, four, or six units. No consistent pattern emerges in comparing leader-chorus phrase lengths within a single piece. A pattern does emerge in the number of vowels used in corresponding call-and-response phrases. In Jump Dance I, for example, the leader employs three vowel sounds *(o, a, e)*, and the chorus utilizes these three vowels. In Jump Dance III, the leader sings differing vowels *(o, e, a)*, but their number corresponds with that observed in the choral part *(o, i, a)*. All choral phrases terminate with the vowel /a/; the majority of solo phrases also end with this vowel, the substitution of the vowel /e/ being the only departure from this pattern (see Jump Dances I and III). In all but one dance, the first syllable in the response part is "yo." If this syllable does not appear in the initial position in solo phrases, it normally occurs within the vocable pattern. The only change in this context occurs in example 5.4, which introduces a new vocable pattern.

The sum of vowels in both parts is four: *a, e, I, o*. Comparison of the leader and chorus syllables including these vowels may be diagrammed as follows:

leader:	ha	na	ya	he	le	we	bi	hi	li	o	ho	yo
chorus:	ha	na	ya	he	le		bi	hi	li			yo

Thus, there is a close correspondence between the vocables found in each part.

This brief examination of some specific Choctaw songs infers that meaning appears to be ascribed at the level of /piece/, rather than at the level of /phrase/ (in Euro-American terms). The lack of meaningful text leads one to look at gross levels of meaning, in contrast to the level of /phrase/. The *amona tuluwa* is obviously an indicator of importance; if my theory is correct, the Jump Dances are also significant markers for the beginning of a cycle. If these pieces serve as "indicators," then the question arises: are they something more?

One is dealing with abstractions, both in the *amona tuluwa* and in the Jump dance. There is no counterpart in the phenomenal world, no metaphorical correlation to real life. Hence, any semantic attribution becomes meaningless. No Choctaw consultant or singer has been able to verbalize about the meaning of these pieces. It is possible that a semantic component, once existent, has been forgotten, or was initially hidden and subsequently forgotten. This argument, however, seems to be specious.

In Choctaw ideology, and apparently in other Native American societies, animal symbols reflect nontangible, nonphenomenal energies. The Choctaw, especially individuals in the role of shaman, seem to be aware of types of energy that normally escape the human sensory receivers. For the most part, animal dances are abstract statements about this "other" reality or concept of reality. Animal dances, then, do not function in metaphorical relationships with their earthly counterparts. The latter are simply a means of rendering the world of spirits, or spirit energies, understandable. Given this background, we may assume that the songs under consideration in this article may be functioning in the same manner.

Many ethnomusicologists, as well as other Western scholars, have given little credence to the mystical, metaphysical domains of American Indian thought. Yet, indeed, it is in this sphere of proposed "reality" that we must examine these pieces if we are to establish their semantic level. This is also true for Native American music in general.

Occasions for the performance of Indian music are indeed transcendent in nature. Outsiders should be aware of this phenomenon in performance contexts. One feels compelled to ask why Western scholars have not pursued research in this area. I expect that we shall determine the semantic component when we have adequate methods to examine the metaphysical aspects of this music.

Notes

Fieldwork among the Mississippi Choctaw was initiated in 1969, with the aid of a National Defense Education Act Fellowship through Tulane University. Faculty grants from the California State University Foundation at Bakersfield, the Institute of American Cultures, and the American Indian Studies Center at UCLA have enabled me to continue with this research.

1. See Howard and Levine 1990. After James H. Howard's untimely death, his widow refused to allow Victoria Lindsay Levine to make any corrections to the parts of the manuscript he had completed, including obvious errors. For specific examples of Howard's errors, see my review of the monograph (Draper 1992).

2. For a comparison with Oklahoma Choctaw music, see Levine 1993, 1997a, and 1997b.

3. Choctaw terms follow, when relevant, the orthography observed in existing

works. This is primarily for the convenience of readers referring to earlier publications. The translations of Choctaw terms were provided by my consultants.

4. The dance formation of the *tinsanale hitkla* corresponds with the current Wedding Dance, although the Choctaw title has changed. I have been unable to obtain a recording of a *tinsanale hitkla,* and therefore am persuaded to conclude that these dances are the same.

5. The dance movements of the Jump Dance follow the description of Frances Densmore's Stomp Dance (1943). The latter term is one that the older Choctaw singers do not recognize; thus, it implies Densmore's designation.

6. In the semicircular dance formation, men precede women, and participants interlock arms. The dance step include a jumping movement on both feet, with the group moving counterclockwise.

References

Bushnell, David. 1909. *The Choctaw of Bayou Lacombe, St. Tammany Parish, Louisiana.* Bureau of American Ethnology Bulletin 48. Washington, D.C.: U.S. Government Printing Office.

Densmore, Frances. 1943. *Choctaw Music.* Anthropological Paper no. 28. Bureau of American Ethnology Bulletin 136. Washington, D.C.: U.S. Government Printing Office.

Draper, David E. 1971. "Acculturation in Choctaw Indian Music." Paper presented at the Annual Meeting of the Society for Ethnomusicology, Chapel Hill, N.C.

———. 1975. "Folk Categories, Contexts, and Musical Performance." Paper presented at the Annual Meeting of the American Folklore Society, New Orleans.

———. 1992. "Review of Choctaw Music and Dance." *Journal of the Society for Ethnomusicology* 36, no. 3: 416–20.

Howard, James H., and Victoria Lindsay Levine. 1990. *Choctaw Music and Dance.* Norman: University of Oklahoma Press.

Levine, Victoria. 1993. "Musical Revitalization among the Choctaw." *American Music* 11, no. 4: 391–411.

———. 1997a. "Music, Myth, and Medicine in the Choctaw Indian Ballgame." *Enchanting Powers: Music in the World's Religions,* edited by Lawrence Sullivan. Cambridge: Harvard University Center for the Study of World Religion.

———. 1997b. "Text and Context in Choctaw Social Dance Songs." *Florida Anthropologist* 50, no. 4: 183–87.

Peterson, John. 1970. "The Mississippi Band of Choctaw Indians: Their Recent History and Current Social Relations." Ph.D. diss., University of Georgia.

Stevenson, George W. 1976. "The Hymnody of the Choctaw Indians of Oklahoma." Ph.D. diss., Southern Baptist Theological Seminary.

Swanton, John R. 1911. *Indian Tribes of the Lower Mississippi Valley.* Bureau of American Ethnology Bulletin 43. Washington, D.C.: U.S. Government Printing Office.

———. 1931. *Source Material for the Social and Ceremonial Life of the Choctaw Indians.* Bureau of American Ethnology Bulletin 103. Washington, D.C.: U.S. Government Printing Office.

6 "This Is Our Dance"
The Fire Dance of the Fort Sill Chiricahua Warm Springs Apache

T. CHRISTOPHER APLIN

The Fort Sill Chiricahua Warm Springs Apache are their Fire Dance. That is to say, the dance represents them as a collective people because it bears the marks of their culture, history, and identity. The Fire Dance expresses their religious outlook while simultaneously celebrating their exuberance and joy in simply living. It is sacred and social, reverent and bawdy, feast and fellowship, athletic and poetic, men and women, humor and beauty. A study of this ceremony reveals the process of change that has shaped the character of the modern Fort Sill Apache tribe and its members. Like the Apache themselves, the Fire Dance has been the subject of sensational portrayal in the writings and perceptions of cultural outsiders, and—fair or unfair—these portrayals have shaped in varying degrees their own perception of themselves. In order to grasp the nuances of this sacred ceremonial practice and its overall embodiment of the tribe's unique characteristics, it is first necessary to understand some general background about the multifaceted Fort Sill Apache themselves, as well as some basic details about the dance.

The Fort Sill Chiricahua Warm Springs Apache: A Brief History

The Fort Sill Apache are, of course, first and foremost culturally *Apaches.* They are part of a larger fabric of southwestern Apachean groups such as the Western, Jicarilla, Lipan, and Mescalero Apaches, who share a related Athapaskan linguistic background. With other Athapaskan speakers in the American Southwest, they also share some similarities in religious outlook, often expressed through the performance of masked-dance ceremonials such as the Fire Dance. Due to these regional and tribal ties, the Fort Sill Apache and their dance are significantly marked by southwestern cultural traits.

The Fort Sill Apache are not merely Apaches, but *Chiricahua* Apaches. As such, they represent the confluence of several historically distinct tribal entities, or bands—the Eastern Chiricahua, Chihénde, or Warm Springs Apache; the Central Chiricahua, Cochise Apache, or Chukunen; the Southern Chiricahua, Pinery Apache, or Ndé'ndaí; as well as the Bidanku. Although these bands lived in geographic proximity in what is now Arizona, New Mexico, and northern Mexico, each maintained relative autonomy. These diverse Chiricahua groups were thrown together in the late 1880s, united as much by circumstance as culture, language, or blood.

The late-nineteenth-century struggles of the Fort Sill Apache ancestors in the American Southwest centered on the Chiricahua Apache bands that, due to consolidation policies enacted in the U.S. territories at that time, were forced from their own reservations in southern Arizona and western New Mexico onto the San Carlos Reservation in southeastern Arizona. Rather than resign themselves to reservation existence and the distrust, corruption, and crowding characteristic of San Carlos at that time, famous leaders such as Victorio, Mangus, and Geronimo led factions of the tribe on repeated flights from the reservation in an attempt to maintain control of their own destinies in the mountains of the Southwest and northern Mexico. The supply raids on area settlements and military conflict that accompanied these reservation outbreaks continued until August 1886 when the Chiricahua were—depending on one's perspective—compelled, tricked, or required due to inadequate supplies to surrender to the U.S. military.

Although it is clear that one monolithic tribal identity does not exist, it is safe to say that this violent history in the Southwest has come to stand as an emblem of Chiricahua identity for tribal outsiders. For regional settlers, military forces, early historians, and later Hollywood, the Chiricahua often represented violence and war. Typifying this interpretation of Chiricahua culture, historian Frank C. Lockwood states, "Tradition attributes great cruelty to the Apache. . . . [M]arauding and murdering, they were . . . the most disconcerting and harassing of enemies" (Lockwood and Thrapp 1987: 5). Even other Apachean and Native American communities commonly associate the Chiricahua with this period of violence, but they often attach an inverse meaning: cultural resistance and leadership. The continuing currency of this interpretation of Chiricahua history and culture manifests itself in diverse ways in broader American Indian popular culture. In the 1998 movie *Smoke Signals*, the Coeur d'Alene protagonist, Victor, during a break in a basketball game, states—laced with dry humor and perhaps admiration—that the best basketball player ever was Geronimo because "he was lean, mean, and bloody." A notable sight at recent intertribal pow-wows is a T-shirt featuring a photograph of Geronimo with three other Chiricahua, bearing the words: "Homeland Security: Fighting Terrorism since 1492."

Following their submission in 1886, members of the Chiricahua bands became prisoners of war for a period of twenty-seven years; during this period of relocation and imprisonment, popular culture and history texts largely lose sight of the Apache prisoners. Academic writings about this period of incarceration in the East in Florida and Alabama and later at Fort Sill, Oklahoma, often ascribe to the Chiricahua the identity of victim—victim of government policy, cultural loss through assimilative policy, and illness through maltreatment. Perhaps more important throughout this period of upheaval, they were apparent cultural negotiators, or survivors, holding on to cultural elements deemed central to their continuance as a people, while also adopting or adapting as they always had to outside languages, religions, and medical practices.

Their enforced relocation made the Chiricahua the only southwestern group living in diaspora in the East. Once entrenched in Oklahoma in 1894, they were given a new name, the "Geronimo," or Fort Sill Apache, and an identity of greater complexity. Of the 498 Chiricahua originally sent to Florida, only 237 living members remained upon their 1913 release from prisoner-of-war status at Fort Sill. There they were a small southwestern isolate amid a larger Native American community that, then as today, is predominantly composed of more populous eastern woodland and central plains Indians. Further, the small group of prisoners, also then as now, lives within a larger Native American and Euro-American community characterized by an economic reliance on the local Fort Sill military base and strong adherence to various forms of Protestant Christian theology. These new cultural influences brought with them new relationships, exchanges, and responsibilities that shaped the Fort Sill Apache as they in turn contributed to the overall character of the regional community.

By 1913 the "Fort Sill Apache," as they had come to be known, had experienced more than two generations in captivity and the death of Geronimo. Freed tribe members were allowed the option of either receiving land allotments near the military post or relocating once again to the Mescalero reservation located in New Mexico, near Ruidoso.[1] Approximately two-thirds of the tribe accepted a place with their Mescalero relatives. The handful that remained in southwest Oklahoma after the group split in 1913 continued their lives as a small but distinct cultural group within the southern plains region. Tribal members penned and ratified a constitution in the 1970s, received two federal land-claims settlement awards for their lost ancestral lands in Arizona and New Mexico, formally organized their tribal government, and the Geronimo or Fort Sill Apaches transformed once again, this time known as the Fort Sill Apache Tribe of Oklahoma. Many still reside in southwestern Oklahoma, north of the military post of their earlier confinement, near a town called Apache, Oklahoma.

Fire Dance Overview

The Fire Dance remained a cultural constant throughout the Fort Sill Apache transition period of the late 1800s and early 1900s, traveling with them from the Southwest, through years of imprisonment, and into the modern day. Whereas history books and popular culture sometimes generalize the Apache with characterizations ranging from renegade to freedom fighter and victim to survivor, an exploration of the Fire Dance reveals a broader spectrum of identity in Fort Sill Apache culture. Through the dance, they are revealed as a tribe of religious reflection and ideals, creativity and tradition, artisans and craftsmen. In order to get closer to the dance and its meaning to the modern Fort Sill Apache, we must first have a clear understanding of the background and elements of the ceremony.

The masked ceremonial dance common among the Apache tribes of the Southwest has been known by different names throughout the history of its documentation. Early ethnographers fascinated by the spectacular visual image of its performance dubbed the rite the Devil Dance. Still others have classified it as the Horn Dance, a reference to the physical similarity between the headdress and deer antlers. Anthropologist Morris Edward Opler dubbed it the Dance of the Mountain Spirits (1941). The numerous terminologies for this ceremony stem in part from the fact that most Athapaskan-speaking groups of the Southwest practice it in diverse form. Distantly related is the Yeibechei ceremony of the Navajo and the Háschín of the Jicarilla, whereas the Western Apache Crown Dance, the Mescalero Dance of the Mountain Gods, and the Fire Dance of the Fort Sill Chiricahua Warm Springs Apache are more closely related.

The introduction of the Fire Dance ceremony to the Chiricahua and Warm Springs Apache is documented in local oral tradition, given as a gift from the Gahe to aid the tribe in times of need. The recipient of the ceremony was deemed a medicine man. This individual traditionally coordinated dance performances, which were conducted over a four-day period, to heal the sick or in conjunction with what is commonly referred to as the girl's puberty rite. In both past and present, performance of the Fire Dance is reflective of both the religious beliefs and the social practices of the Fort Sill Apache. Whether held for healing purposes, celebrating the passage of a young girl into womanhood, or simply to bestow blessings upon its performers and audience, this dance commences at twilight as the sun sinks below the western horizon, unfolds around a bonfire, and is performed by masked dancers to the accompaniment of music.

Central to the performance of the dance are the Gahe, a race of beneficent beings who live in the mountains. The Gahe are among the most developed characters within Apache religious belief. These beings often number four—the black Gahe for the East, the blue Gahe of the South, the yellow Gahe of the West, and the white Gahe of the North. Although they bring health, protection, and blessings to the Fort Sill Apache, their power is also feared. Accordingly, these figures were traditionally addressed indirectly with the term *Chazhááda,* or "pointed hats," as a sign of respect (M. Darrow interview, April 4, 2002).[2] Other forms of avoidance or deference to the Gahe such as not touching them or imitating their characteristic call similarly display respect for their power. Origin stories of the Chiricahua record disease and death among the consequences of disrespecting the Gahe (see Opler 1942: 79; Hoijer 1938: 30–33). As beings of both kindness and, when provoked, wrath, the Gahe interact with the Chiricahua in an evolving relationship that displays emotions of a human nature.

As the Fort Sill dancers perform the Fire Dance, they do so in accordance with the way taught them by the Gahe. The Gahe headdress typically consists of a black buckskin or canvas mask that covers the dancer's face and vertical and horizontal slats of wood, in the shape of a trident, perched atop the head. The upper body of each dancer is adorned in painted designs, heavy buckskin kilts cover the lower body until approximately mid- to lower calf, and bootlike moccasins that, in accordance with Chiricahua tradition have characteristic upturned toes, are worn on the feet. Their outfits may be accented further with bells or jingles, cloth streamers, or feather ornaments. In addition, each of the Gahe dancers typically carries two sword-shaped slats, one in each hand, as he moves about the dance area performing the high step, or another of their three characteristic dance steps.

The recurrence of important religious concepts (specifically, reference made to the cardinal directions and ritual repetition of action by four) adds a sense of unity to the performance. These interrelated concepts—evident in the origin stories associated with the dance, repetition of songs, regalia design, and actions, for example—are evident throughout the historical documentation of the dance and in modern performances. Regarding the symbolic meaning of the number four within some Apache belief, Western Apache scholar Thomas L. Larson counts among its meanings unity, inclusiveness, and balance, and anchors it to observable manifestations in day-to-day human life: the four directions, the four seasons, and the four elements of fire, earth, wind, and air. Larson notes that, in giving a blessing with a pinch of pollen, an Apache "draws a cross in the air above the head and then draws an imaginary circle around it, signifying the four directions unified by the circle, or universe" (1996: 169). Claire R. Farrer, who has worked among Mescalero Apache groups since the 1960s, confirms in part Larson's interpretation. When speaking of the number four, or what she calls "the base metaphor," she states that the number four represents balance, circularity, and directionality (1980: 147).

The Gahe are assisted, within both oral tradition and modern performance, by a figure known as Gray One. Anthropologists of Southwest ceremonies commonly refer to figures such as Gray One as a ceremonial clown. His role within the Fire Dance ceremony is in fact often as a prankster or joker, yet his powers are respected and sometimes even greater than those of the Gahe. The clowns dress in a distinctive manner, wearing a pair of cutoff shorts, their full bodies painted white, with white canvas masks accented by angular noses and ears. Though a powerful figure within the ceremonial, it is young novice males who typically perform this role, practicing for the day they will become Gahe dancers.

The Fire Dance of the Fort Sill Chiricahua Warm Springs Apache is a complex performance practice because it is a ritual that rests at the intersection of religion and medicine, oral tradition and visual artistry, dance and drama, history and modern life. The use of music adds further depth to this dense mixture. Rather than simply ornamenting or embellishing the ceremony, the Fire Dance songs that typically accompany the dance, called *gahe biyine* in the Chiricahua language (M. Darrow interview, April 4, 2002), provide the rhythm and energetic drive for the event. These songs coordinate the angular movements of the individual dancers and Gahe groups, allowing for proper execution of the ceremony. Although most Fort Sill Apaches no longer speak their traditional language fluently, the lyrical sections of Fire Dance songs are the most overt communicators to those event attendees equipped to decode its communicative meaning—whether local Fort Sill Apache, visiting Mescalero or Western Apaches, or other closely related Athapaskan speakers. Music, though only a component part of a greater whole, is the fulcrum around which the other elements elaborate.

Each group of Gahe dancers has an associated group of musicians. Time is kept on a water drum held in the crook of the arm. The drums seen at modern Fire Dance performances are often metal pots with an inner tube or buckskin stretched over the mouth, acting as the drumhead.

In the past, young novice Apache boys played along, crowding around a flat piece of rawhide, beating out the rhythm simultaneously. The rhythm for the dance, usually a straight quarter-note beat or sometimes a pulsing eighth-note beat, is created by striking a drumstick with a small hoop on the distal end against the drumhead. Jingles, bells, and small wooden sticks adorning the dancers' headdresses also contribute to the rhythmic texture.

Though variation is common, the number of singers in a group generally ranges between four and six. The melody is typically a heterophonic line, sung by a male chorus. The head singer begins each song by singing solo a small portion of the melody. Once the other performers recognize the song, they join in. Although subtle variations in form are apparent, the melodic organization of Fire Dance melodies fall under two main categories: a binary strophic form (A/B) and a strophic form (repeated A). These melodic sections are sung in vocables and, in the most generalized form, are often alternated with a contrasting section composed of a speech-song recitation of text,[3] a prayer uttered in the traditional Chiricahua language (A B/C or repeated A/B).[4]

The Contemporary Annual Fire Dance of the Fort Sill Apache

The Fire Dance began as an organizationally promoted and annually celebrated event for the Fort Sill Chiricahua Warm Springs Apache in 1980. This event at present takes place every September, roughly coinciding with the dedication of the Fort Sill Chiricahua Warm Springs tribal complex and, coincidentally, the same month of Geronimo's final negotiation to General Nelson Miles in 1886. These annual Fire Dance performances fit broadly into a consistent format. Festivities begin after the workday on Friday evening and last until early Sunday morning. The Friday performance often commences with a Gourd Dance at around six thirty in the evening, with the Gahe dancers taking over the dance ground soon after sundown. The Saturday celebration is usually an all-day affair and might include events such as a horseshoe tournament, an Apache War Dance demonstration, a reception for the Apache tribal princess, lectures by Fort Sill Apache tribal historian Michael Darrow, a communal dinner, and more Gourd Dancing. The Gahe dancers again take control of the dance area soon after sundown and usually perform until sometime around midnight. Round Dances and Back-and-Forth Dances—both traditional social song-and-dance forms of the Chiricahua Warm Springs Apache—follow the Gahe Dance.

The Fort Sill Chiricahua Warm Springs tribal headquarters, the site of the annual celebration, is located on Route 2, just north of Apache in southwestern Oklahoma. A visitor to this multiple-unit facility will notice on the north side of the grounds a gymnasium and the office building for the Fort Sill Chiricahua Warm Springs Tribal Housing Authority. Across the asphalt parking lot and to the southwest of this structure is a building housing a kitchen, a communal area, and a small exhibit highlighting the historic saga of the Chiricahua Warm Springs Apache. Beyond this site to the south are the main offices of the tribal headquarters. Located just to the east of these structures is an emergency youth shelter and, on the southeasternmost portion of the complex, the dance area where the September Fire Dance festivities unfold every year.

Walking behind the youth shelter and into the dance area during the September celebration, a first-time attendee may be struck by a myriad of images, sounds, and smells. Circling the dance ground are minivans, SUVs, trucks, and sedans of all varieties. Vendors set up booths and market their wares. On the south and north sides of the dance grounds, food sales are earned by pedaling such treats as sodas, cheese-drenched nachos, and Indian fry bread. Beadwork and other crafts are also common items. A booth selling T-shirts featuring the Fort Sill Chiricahua Warm Springs name and a stylized depiction of a Gahe dancer, an image created by famed Fort Sill Apache artist Alan Houser, is usually located on the northwestern portion of the dance ground. When the weather cooperates, craftspeople unload their goods at a healthier pace than on the damper, more sparsely attended evenings of the dance.

Event spectators line the outer ring of the dance ground, some perched on wooden benches beneath a long, slender semicircular arbor, others sitting in the open, atop the ubiquitous foldout chair so common at Native American events in Oklahoma, or on blankets stretched out on the ground. There are many happy greetings, pats on the back, and reunions with visiting relatives. The event draws a diverse crowd. Though the English language—as opposed to the "complex" Apache, the "matter-of-fact" Comanche, or the "sing-song, drawling" tones of the Kiowa once noted by the early 1900s ethnographer M. R. Harrington (1912: 9)—has emerged as the lingua franca among attendees, the demographic makeup of the yearly dance is still predominantly composed of local Fort Sill or visiting Mescalero Apache, in combination with other area tribes such as the Kiowa, Comanche, and Plains Kiowa-Apache, or Wichita, Caddo, and Delaware.

Children chase each other; in one instance, a young boy clutched a younger counterpart with an unbreakable headlock, while the smaller victim wiggled in a vain attempt to escape. Teens often wander the outer circle, some dressed in Tommy Hilfiger clothing and baseball caps with meticulously curved brims, others with spiked hair and flared pants, often with the ever present cell phone prominently displayed, sizing up the scene. Adults at the event may be dressed in regalia typical of the Plains-based Gourd Dance, others in jeans and sneakers, sweatshirts, cowboy hats, and miscellaneous traditional accessories. A significant portion of the audience sits quietly—big and small, young and old, Native American, Euro-American, mixed Native and Euro-American, University of Oklahoma exchange students, and lifelong Okie alike—waiting for the main attraction as the pink and orange southwestern Oklahoma sky yields to growing darkness and the emerging stars.

The Fire Dance segments of these tribal celebrations generally consist of three sections: an introduction, a main body, and a conclusion. Local and visiting dancers first initiate the ceremony in an introductory segment during which each group enters the dance area at separate times—and completely independent of each other—and consecrates the dance area by blessing the four directions.

After the introduction, all Gahe groups exit the dance grounds to the east. The all-male drummers and singers move into position near the western perimeter and seat themselves on a long bench made from cinder blocks and planks of wood. Each drummer cradles a small, round water drum, perhaps eight to twelve inches in diameter, in the crook of his left arm. In his right hand he holds a drumstick of approximately six to eight inches. A hoop of approximately one to two inches in diameter adorns the tip of the stick, striking the drum membrane. Their drumbeat provides the pulse for the duration of the evening.

As the musicians prepare for their performance, female dancers form a parallel line behind them. Groups of women might line up along the outer northeast and southeast perimeter as well. Each female dancer wears a shawl laced with long fringe. A group of Gahe dancers reenters the dance ground for the main body of the evening celebration, makes a full clockwise lap around the dance circle, blesses each of the four directions, and stops on the western side of the fire immediately in front of the musicians. The other Gahe dancer groups enter the dance area and follow approximately the same procedure.

Once the musicians and dancers are in place, the musicians initiate the beat. The single voice of the head singer breaks through the air, and the chorus of male vocalists immediately follows his lead. Local Fort Sill and visiting Mescalero groups each have a corresponding group of musicians with their own distinctive style and repertoire. These groups of approximately four to six musicians rotate throughout the evening, sharing in the responsibility of providing accompaniment for the dancers. The beats that drive the evening performance are composed of a straight quarter-note rhythmic pattern or a subdivided eighth-note pattern.

The rhythmic pattern of the beat signals to the Gahe the appropriate dance step. Taking their cues from their lead dancer, the remaining dancers quickly join in. Moving in a clockwise motion around the fire, the Gahe dancers make sharp turns and strike dramatic poses. Sometimes moving toward the fire, sometimes away, the dancers often bend over at the waist, nodding or shaking their heads slightly. The percussive sticks on the headdress and bells on their kilts accent the rhythm of these movements. The dancers' wands are held in their palms, often pointed away from the body, or flipped back, resting on the forearms. At times, a dancer extends his arms from his shoulder toward the sky, and calls out into the night.

The groups of women on the outer ring of the dance site move slowly with a gentle kicking step around the perimeter. Their left feet emphasize the downbeat. Watching the movement of their feet, holding a small child, or simply observing the dance scene before them, they shuffle clockwise around the circular dance area.

The dance continues this way for some time, occupying the majority of the evening. The Gahe dance segment typically commences at approximately nine o'clock and does not conclude until around midnight. If the women fatigue, they take a break by walking off the dance area. The Gahe take frequent breaks as well, and if a male dancer wants to rest, he raises his wands as he exits on the east side. At times, an entire group can exit the dance area, with the leader steering the group off the ground, and all dancers raising their wands together as a unanimous "Ohhhhh!" is called out to the east.

The musicians are not immune to the strains of performance, either. After the completion of a song, a small pause is often observed before moving to the next. When this happens, the Gahe dancers suspend their dancing and trot around the dance area, calling out to the singers as they pass until the music is resumed.

The Fire Dance and the Continuity of Change

Documents record Fire Dance practices dating from at least the 1880s, though it is certain that the dance was performed long before that date. Written records such as the following often reflect the evolutionary thinking of nontribal outsiders, yet they document recognizable elements of the Fire Dance:

[The Apache] have medicine men who are allowed no fees from patients. Colds and consumption are about all the complaints the Apaches suffer from. If the patient is very sick, past being benefited by herbs or root, they have a grand medicine dance, continuing it for 6 or 7 days. They commence this strange performance about sunset. The medicine man with four or five others go into the neighboring hills, making their appearance at times whooping to those in camp. These are employed in chanting a single melody and keeping time by rasping a notched stick with one that is held in the hand. A large fire is built in front of the one in which are seated the singers. After a time the medicine men make their appearance with curious headdresses, around the bottom of which feathers are fastened extending over and covering the face. Their backs, breasts, and legs are painted with red and black zig-zag lines. They come in, dance around the fire led by a fellow whose actions resemble the monkey antics of a clown. He is dressed less gaudily than the others. They circle two or three times around the fire and off they go to appear in a few moments going through the same strange performance whilst dancing about the fires. Each gives an unearthly yell at the same time turning to face one another. These nightly dances continue until the patient declares him or herself better. This I presume they would say even on the point of death. (Higgins n.d.: 16–18)

The common use of adjectives such as *strange, curious,* and *gaudy* in ethnographic documents expresses some degree of condescension on the part of the writers, or at least strong aesthetic aversion, and reinforces the characteristics of violence and war attributed to the Apache and the Chiricahua in particular. Regardless of its subjectivity, this event description remains historically important for its clear depiction of a Fire Dance–related practice: a multiday ceremony led by a medicine man, with masked dancers, accompanying music, and symbolic emphasis on the number four, held for healing purposes.

The Fire Dance accompanied the Fort Sill Apache throughout their struggles in the late eighteenth and early nineteenth centuries. Historical accounts tell of its performance by the Apache prisoners of war in both St. Augustine and Pensacola. As the imprisoned Apaches at Fort Marion fell ill due to the unhealthful coastal climate and cramped living conditions, they improvised a Gahe dance with whatever materials they could find in their new home. When the prisoners departed from Florida, they left behind a picture of a Fire Dance Gahe etched into the walls of the old Spanish fort.

The Fire Dance persisted through a ban placed on its performance during the Fort Sill Apache's imprisonment in Oklahoma at the turn of the twentieth century. While simultaneously struggling with the medical afflictions that began in the East and the influence of Dutch Reformed missionaries, they held Fire Dances with increased interest, often performing them outdoors in the cold of winter. The ban, initiated by the commanding officers in charge of the Fort Sill Apache, lasted only until around 1900 or 1901, and the extent of its enforcement cannot be stated definitively based on available material. This particular event is significant, however, in that it is a nephew of Geronimo, a converted Christian educated at Carlisle Indian School, who claims at least partial responsibility for this limited ban on the dance.

While historically documented events attest to the long-standing practice and importance of the Fire Dance to the Fort Sill Apache culture, they also document a process of adaptation and change for the tribe in new religious, medical, and regional contexts. The medicine man, called *di-yin* in the Chiricahuan language, was an important and influential member of the tribe and key to the perpetuation of the Fire Dance tradition. This local dignitary was responsible not only for tribal medical well-being but also their spiritual well-being. The introduction of Western medical practices and Christian missionaries to the Fort Sill Apache represented a dual challenge to the influence of the medicine man.

Still other influences shaped the Fire Dance over time. As with other Native tribes, an important cultural link was compromised through the loss of the traditional language as youth were sent to boarding schools. This erosion of language was perhaps more dramatic for the Fort Sill Apache due to their small population and isolated residence amid other Native, predominantly plains, cultures. Numerous other influences might be counted to attest to changes in Fire Dance performance: new intertribal musical practices, or the proliferation of American popular music; intertribal marriage and adoption of woodlands, plains, or intertribal social and ceremonial practices; the geographic distance of the Fort Sill Apache from their regional and cultural neighbors after the tribal separation of 1913; or the severed link between traditional modes of occupation, transition to an agricultural economy as promoted by governmental policy, and finally the modern workweek. Yet there is still the Fire Dance.

Gahe Biyine Prayers and the Transmission of Religious Ideals

Dr. Michael Steck, Indian agent to the Apache tribes of the Southwest in the 1850s, once emphasized the communicative divide between Apache musical practice and the aesthetics of the recently arrived Euro-American population when he commented on the "absurd" custom of the girl's puberty ceremony, in which "the parents at this feast will sacrifice all the property they possess to feast the tribe, who dance and make *night hideous with their songs"* (Steck cited in Thrapp 1974: 86; emphasis in the original). Steck's language use parallels other historical documents of Apache musical and ceremonial performance in the late 1800s, emphasizing perceptions of violence or savagery. Had his writings taken into consideration the lyrical prayers central to Fire Dance song, his written depictions may have been quite different in character.

Gahe biyine—or the songs that accompany Fire Dance performance—have a very specific and important purpose, namely, petitioning the Gahe for their blessings and assistance. Harry Hoijer's *Chiricahua and Mescalero Apache Texts* (1938) is an important ethnographic document that records, in the Chiricahua and English languages, the stories and song texts of relocated Fort Sill Apache elders residing at the Mescalero Reservation. In a footnote to the translated text, Hoijer states, "Songs . . . are sung by the shaman [or medicine man] when he is preparing the dancers and while they are dancing. These songs function as a message to the Mountain Spirits to acquaint them of the aid required by the shaman. Since they are the songs which the Mountain Spirits themselves taught the shaman, it is believed that they must respond to them" (154).

These songs are constructed with contrasting sections. The first of these is the main sung melody. Rather than having strict literary meaning, these sections are instead sung with abstracted vocables. The second section of the song is the speech-song vocal recitation, or spoken prayer. These sections include text, or prayers in the traditional Chiricahua language. Lyrical content often emphasizes important symbolic concepts to the Apache, including reference to the Gahe, their mountain home, clouds or earth, and ceremonial items of importance such as turquoise, abalone shell, or pollen.

The following verse, taken from Hoijer's work, is a translation of a *gahe biyine* prayer that displays some traits typical of these passages.[5] Apparent in the text is a lyrical convention typical of many *gahe biyine* texts, namely, the frequent reference to color and directional associations of the Gahe at the beginning of each line of text (M. Darrow interview, April 4, 2002). Written under the heading "Songs of the Mountain Spirit Ceremony," the English translation of the lyrical verse reads:

> Big Blue Mountain Spirit in the east,
> The tassels of the earth are moving about with me,
> Here, my songs have been created,
>
> Big Yellow Mountain Spirit in the south,
> Leader of the Mountain Spirits, holy Mountain Spirit,
> He will ask for the good life for us,
> Here, my songs have again been created,

Big White Mountain Spirit in the west,
Leader of the Mountain Spirits, holy Mountain Spirit,
For this reason, my songs have been created,

Big Black Mountain Spirit in the north,
Leader of the Mountain Spirits, holy Mountain Spirit,
My songs will go out to the four directions.
   (Hoijer 1938: 54)[6]

Note that there are four complete stanzas—an address for each of the four Gahe, their four color designations, as well as reference to each of the four cardinal directions.

Hoijer interprets the phrase "the tassels of the earth" as synonymous in meaning to "the pollen of the earth" (1938: 154–55). Pollen is considered a ceremonial or sacred item and is multifaceted in its potential meaning. It is thought to represent health and vigor, growth and vitality. Extending the possible meaning of pollen within Fire Dance ceremony and song, pollen is linked to the color yellow and to the ceremony by the yellow Gahe, or in the case of this lyrical example, the Gahe of the South. Further, pollen can represent the sun and, by extension, God or God's generosity, or have ties to the female (Larson, 1996: 205). Due to the prominent use of pollen within the girl's puberty rite, pollen as a sacred substance also may be connected to ideas of fertility.

Pollen as a symbol in Apache religious belief certainly has many meanings, and it is partially in these deeper realms of interpretation that the Fire Dance and its song become the embodiment of Apache belief and worldview—Fort Sill, Mescalero, or otherwise. Fort Sill Apache tribal historian Michael Darrow links the phrase to the properties of pollen— abundance, fruitfulness, and life. He states further that if the "tassels of the earth," or pollen, were "moving about with you," then "everything in the world is . . . surrounding you and is causing everything to be that much better. There is goodness everywhere" (interview, April 4, 2002). From that point, the phrase transcends its status as an abstract yet poetic expression, accumulating additional layers of meaning as a commentary on greater human existence. A statement reflective of the values embedded within Fire Dance text, it transforms into a message of doing good things, creating good things, and carrying good ideas with you—having the tassels of the earth move about with you—so that life will be abundant and "goodness" will attain "everywhere."

Such statements and their interpretation according to the individual who processes them are highly subjective. Analysis of such facets of performance can be a powerful indicator of community meanings behind Fire Dance practice, however, and the ability of that practice to transmit the ideals, values, and beliefs of that culture. This text, an optimistic philosophical statement recorded by Hoijer circa 1938, is as much the embodiment of the intellectual outlook of that era as preceding generations and easily counteracts notions of the violent or victim, or the "strange" or "gaudy" in Fire Dance performance.

Fire Dance Performance in Postimprisonment Transition

> The term I was thinking of was *validation.* All these other tribes, all these other groups in the vicinity—not just American Indian—have their various events and activities and things where they are sort of expressive of themselves, wallowing in their own culture. And there's very little of anything . . . that occurs that's equivalent to that for Fort Sill Apache. And for this event that we have, it's the closest we can get to that—something that we can do that's for us. Everything else is always somebody else's. And I'm not sure that most people are aware of what it's like to be existing in a world where everything is somebody else's and the connection is different than what might . . . exist in a situation where you can be surrounded by things that you feel more of a connection with.
>
> —Michael Darrow, Fort Sill Chiricahua Warm Springs tribal historian

A developed picture of Fire Dance performance during the prisoner-of-war years and postimprisonment period (1913–present) has yet to be fully realized. With the majority of the population choosing to relocate in 1913, the tribal split between Oklahoma and New Mexico created a considerable strain on the ability of the Fort Sill group to maintain the cultural infrastructure for consistent performance and perpetuation of the Fire Dance ceremony. Some feeling remains in the tribe today that the relocation of prominent Fort Sill leaders and dance enthusiasts strengthened the Fire Dance tradition on the Mescalero Reservation. Locally in Oklahoma, "visitations," or informal family get-togethers featuring a supper and backyard, basement, or kitchen singing of Fire Dance, Round Dance, and Back-and-Forth Dance songs without the accompanying dances, may have been a important mode of performance during both the imprisonment and parts of the postimprisonment periods.

With a small postimprisonment population, few singers and dancers, and limited occasions and venues for the ceremony, performance of the Fire Dance after 1912 is perhaps best characterized as intermittent. In a tradition that endures still today, a local Fort Sill Apache family started performing annually at the Anadarko Indian Exposition in the 1940s. Aside from informal "visitation" sings, full dance performances occurred only as the occasion arose—for the annual exposition, various family celebrations, upon special request or invitation of other area tribes, and on at least one occasion for healing purposes. Sometimes these Fire Dance celebrations lasted for the traditional four days.

An annual Fire Dance celebration was established in 1980 for the reorganized Fort Sill Chiricahua Warm Springs Apache tribe. The institution of the dance as an annual event linked the dance to an established, centralized political body, bringing with it a new role for the ceremony as the most visible outward manifestation of an official Fort Sill Apache culture. This new status for the Fire Dance is only one change of many over the past century. The Fire Dance in Oklahoma is no longer performed over the traditional four-day period. The display of respect for the Gahe through avoidance has largely disappeared. Also, the sacred ceremony is no longer held for the purposes of healing or to honor a girl's puberty rite. It is perhaps in part because of the separation of the dance from these important rites that local discussion on the Fire Dance sometimes indicates that tribal members perceive a loss of "significance"—ritual, spiritual, or otherwise—as generations progressed throughout the twentieth century.

Regardless of the debate, the dance continued to perform an important function for members of the Fort Sill Apache over the course of the twentieth century, as it does now at the turn of the millennium. The role of the dance as a vehicle for tribal history, values, and beliefs, or, in the words of Michael Darrow, as a symbol of validation for the Fort Sill Apache (interview, April 4, 2002), makes it a cultural practice of central importance to the tribe and contributed to the establishment of its yearly performance at the tribal headquarters in 1980.

Modern Meaning and the Fire Dance

> The meaning involved with this—the essence of the dance—is a combination of the songs and the posturing of the dancers, and it is all in reverence to our one God, the one . . . whose teachings we follow, or by whom we live. Because that is his name—it's not God—but it is the one we follow, like good and bad, and evil and all this. It's not something you write down; it is something you know. You talk about lie, cheat, steal. Well, that goes on in many cultures, but it is very strong in ours, too. That dance just represents all that is good and all that is holy about us and our people. I feel very

strongly about it because I have grown up, and I was taught that way. It bothers me if I see somebody doing something that they shouldn't be doing . . . let's say a long time ago something that they shouldn't have been doing. But now they have relaxed a lot of the rules, and I want people to see this [Fire Dance] as something that is truly a reverent and spiritual exercise.

—*Ruey Darrow, former Fort Sill Chiricahua Warm Springs Apache tribal chair*

The Fire Dance has multiple meanings for the diverse inhabitants of southwestern Oklahoma. To an outsider looking in, the Gahe may represent to a non-Apache something mysterious and powerful; for a non-Apache child it may represent something foreboding and scary. On the extreme end of this scale, local knowledge around the Fort Sill Apache tribal office tells of the laying of hands upon a youth who mistakenly wore a T-shirt with a depiction of a Gahe dancer on it to a local Christian church meeting. Reflecting on his exposure to the dance as a youth, an urban-dwelling American Indian who grew up in southwestern Oklahoma noted that, in his earliest memory, the Fire Dance was "magical . . . mesmerizing." The frequent depiction of Gahe dancers in the artwork of Kiowa, Comanche, and other area artists attests to the power of its visual imagery and the esteem the dance holds within the regional imagination.

The Fire Dance is an icon to other regional tribes, signifying simply the Fort Sill Apache. Although many nontribal visitors sense the ceremonial or sacred aspects of the dance, their knowledge of its deeper meanings to tribal members may be limited. The annual appearance of Gahe dancers at the Anadarko Indian Exposition—where the dance is performed out of its traditional ceremonial context—may contribute to the perception that the dance has become increasingly secularized.

However, the Fire Dance has, according to tradition, also been a practice that balanced delicately both social and sacred elements. When performed for healing purposes or for a girl's puberty rite, the dance was accompanied by solemn gravity, ritual, and prayer. Yet the dance of the Gahe, both yesterday and today, is often also tied to the performance of the secular Round and Back-and-Forth dances. In the past, boy and girl became boyfriend and girlfriend while dancing as "blanket partners," and these dances lasted until the break of day. The dance movements of the Gahe dancers, though a reverent re-creation of the original dance taught by the *Chazhááda*, are equally expressive of the physical prowess, stamina, and energetic performance style of its dancers.

The term *fellowship* has been used to describe the contemporary function of the annual Fire Dance for the Fort Sill Apache, and it is particularly apt. In many Christian churches, fellowship denotes the period immediately following Sunday services when the congregation can meet and greet each other—on the holiest day of the week, according to Christian theology—while sipping coffee and partaking of sugar-coated pastries. The Fire Dance of the Fort Sill Apache is similar, in that it allows for tribal members to meet, socialize, and catch up while also reflecting on their common religious beliefs as a social community.

The annual Fire Dance is also a homecoming for tribal members. Relatives, friends, and neighbors from the Mescalero reservation in New Mexico, as well as Fort Sill Apaches residing elsewhere throughout the United States, all converge at the tribal headquarters in the latter half of September every year. With hospitality, resident Fort Sill Chiricahua Warm Springs Apache host their guests as they visit, eat, celebrate, partake of organized activities, relax, sing, and dance. Familial relationships are updated, old friendships reaffirmed, and new friendships made. Through these interactions, "tribal members could get together to reassure themselves about who they were" (R. Darrow interview, April 4, 2002).

The modern Fire Dance brings blessings to the Fort Sill Apache through its annual performance. This function of the dance is now often stated as the central purpose for the event, rather than as a healing rite or for a girl's puberty ceremony. Elements of its original function as a healing rite may remain, however, in the words of a local practitioner who attests to the ability of the dance to alleviate fatigue and encourage the elderly into dance. Such statements may, however, simply point to the seemingly universal power of music to uplift—a power that often stems from early memory and a comfort, familiarity, and understanding of the dance and song meaning. Regardless of interpretation, this sentiment affirms the considerable respect paid the dance by local Fort Sill Apache tribal members.

The importance of respect and reverence for the dance is a common refrain of tribal members. For some, respect is shown for the dance through adhering to codes of conduct not only within dance performance but also in day-to-day existence. In this way, the Fire Dance is an important social mechanism in the transmission of behavior. Other tribal members display respect for the dance through emphasizing continuity in the performance of the rite. Whether speaking in terms of consistency in song performance, adherence to traditional taboos, or proper intergenerational transference of a specific dance tradition, it is believed by some that continuity must be maintained across generations through diligent adherence to the ceremony as it was originally received from the Gahe.

The Fort Sill Chiricahua Warm Springs Apache also show their respect for the Fire Dance through protecting the sanctity of its practice. Diverse nontribal people—including hobbyists, Boy Scouts, and academics, as well as other non-Apache Natives—show great curiosity and interest in the Fire Dance ceremony and accompanying songs. Tribal members and performers are aware of the importance of teaching nontribal audience members about their tradition but are often very careful about how much they will talk about the Fire Dance, to whom, and for what purposes. The motivation for this watchful, guarded secrecy is fear of the appropriation, commodification, and diminishment or desecration of a ceremony that holds a sacred and important place within the hearts, minds, and culture of the Fort Sill Chiricahua Warm Springs Apache community.

Throughout their documented history in the Southwest, the Fire Dance has been the continuing cultural thread that reminds the Fort Sill Apache who they are as a cultural group. The dance serves in this self-identification through the transmission of their religious, philosophical, and behavioral ideals, among others. In reminding the tribe to have "the tassels of the earth move about with them," members are encouraged to reflect on their idealized self in a tradition in keeping with their best cultural values. The Fire Dance has also, like the Fort Sill Apache, endured a history of conflict, imprisonment, and relative cultural isolation. In the process, it has been adapted and altered to fit into new contexts and contemporary meanings but never surrendered its unique cultural allegiance. Also, like the Fort Sill Apache, the Fire Dance has meant many things to many people. Whereas early ethnographic documents portrayed the ceremony in a manner that reinforced cultural stereotypes of Apachean violence, the dance today, as it likely has since its earliest performance, represents more clearly "everything that is good and holy" about the Fort Sill Apache. The Fire Dance is a central marker of Fort Sill Chiricahua Warm Spring Apache identity for both tribal insiders and outsiders. As the post-prisoner-of-war generation continues to age, it will be left to the younger generations to maintain the integrity and careful transmission of this important ceremony for those who follow.

Notes

1. The Fort Sill Apache were originally promised ownership of the land upon which the Fort Sill military installation is currently located. The option to receive allotments in Oklahoma was discouraged in large part. Only a small minority of the group received their claims in the state of Oklahoma, often at reduced acreage.

2. The origin and meaning of the term is a matter of debate. Some argue that the term refers to a bird. Both John G. Bourke (1892) and Morris Edward Opler

(1941, 1942, 1983a, 1983b, 1994) use this terminology to refer to the Gahe and the performance of the healing ceremony.

3. The term *vocable* is often defined as sung syllables without dictionary definition.

4. The solidus between the melodic sections (A or A/B) is used to emphasize the distinction between the sung melody and the *sprechstimme*-like textual sections.

5. Analysis of lyrical content may provide some insight into Fort Sill Apache perceptions of religious belief. Ethnologist Harry Hoijer collected his Fire Dance texts from David Fatty (1858–1934), a former Fort Sill Apache prisoner of war then residing at the Mescalero reservation in New Mexico.

6. Note that the color and directional associations listed above are atypical of the most commonly cited Chiricahuan representation—black for the East, blue for the South, yellow for the West, and white for the North (see also Hoijer 1938: 154; Opler 1994: 77n1).

References

Bourke, John G. 1892. *Apache Medicine Men.* Ninth annual report of the Bureau of Ethnology to the secretary of the Smithsonian Institution. Reprint, New York: Dover Publications, 1993.

Darrow, Michael, Fort Sill Apache Tribal Historian. Interview by author, April 4, 2002, Apache, Oklahoma. Tape recording. University of Oklahoma, Norman.

Darrow, Ruey, Fort Sill Chiricahua Warm Spring Apache Tribal Chair. Interview by author, May 2, 2002. Tape recording. University of Oklahoma, Norman.

Farrer, Claire R. 1980. "Singing for Life: The Mescalero Apache Girl's Puberty Ceremony." In *Southwestern Indian Ritual Drama,* edited by Charlotte Frisbee, 129–59. Albuquerque: University of New Mexico Press.

Harrington, M. R. 1912. "The Devil Dance of the Apache." *Museum Journal* (University of Pennsylvania) 3, no. 1: 6–9.

Higgins, N. S. n.d. "Manuscript 180." Smithsonian Institution National Anthropological Archives, Washington, D.C.

Hoijer, Harry. 1938. *Chiricahua and Mescalero Apache Texts: With Ethnological Notes by Morris Edward Opler.* Chicago: University of Chicago Press.

Larson, Thomas LeRoy. 1996. "Gaan/Gahe: The Art and Performance of the Apache Mountain Spirit Dancers." Ph.D. diss., University of California–Santa Barbara.

Lockwood, Frank C., with Dan L. Thrapp. 1987. *The Apache Indians.* Lincoln: University of Nebraska Press.

Opler, Morris Edward. 1941. *An Apache Life-way: The Economic, Social, and Religious Traditions of the Chiricahua Indians.* With introduction by Charles R. Kaut. Chicago: University of Chicago Press. Reprint, Lincoln: University of Nebraska Press, 1996.

———. 1942. *Myths and Tales of the Chiricahua Apache Indians.* With forward by Scott Rushforth. American Folklore Society. Reprint, Lincoln: University of Nebraska Press, 1994.

———. 1983a. "The Apachean Culture Pattern and Its Origins." In *Handbook of North American Indians.* Vol. 10, *Southwest,* general ed. William C. Sturtevant, 368–92. Washington, D.C.: Smithsonian Institution Press.

———. 1983b. "Chiricahua Apache." In *Handbook of North American Indians.*

Vol. 10, *Southwest*, general ed. William C. Sturtevant, 401–18. Washington, D.C.: Smithsonian Institution Press.

———. 1994. *Myths and Tales of the Chiricahua Apache Indians.* American Folklore Society. Reprint, Lincoln: University of Nebraska Press.

Thrapp, Dan L. 1974. *The Conquest of Apacheria.* Norman: University of Oklahoma Press.

7 The Creative Power and Style of Ghost Dance Songs

JUDITH VANDER

The 1890 Ghost Dance, a religious movement originating among the Northern Paiute in Nevada, quickly spread eastward to many tribes on the northern and southern plains. It is easy to imagine the appeal of the religion and its prophecy—destruction of the present world, resurrection of the dead, and immortality in a pristine new world to come—to tribal groups who had been relocated, dislocated, and decimated by illness and warfare. The religion called on its adherents to live peacefully and honestly, and had as its centerpiece the communal performance of song and dance. This was the heart of the religion, the human act that was essential for the fulfillment of its prophecy.

Ghost Dance performance was to take place every six weeks, with dances on four successive nights, the last dance continuing until the morning of the fifth day. Men and women joined hands in a large circle, sidestepping in a clockwise direction while singing Ghost Dance songs. There was no drum or other instrumental accompaniment, only the voices of the dancers joined in unison on each successive Ghost Dance song. At the conclusion of the entire series of Ghost Dances, the dancers feasted and bathed before returning home to ordinary life.

Wovoka, the Northern Paiute prophet who originated the religion, described how he received it from God in a vision: "When the sun died, I went up to heaven and saw God and all the people who had died a long time ago. God told me to come back and tell my people they must be good and love one another, and not fight, or steal, or lie. He gave me this dance to give to my people" (Mooney 1896: 764). This experience took place while Wovoka was sick with fever and lay unconscious, which happened to coincide with a total eclipse of the sun. New converts to the Ghost Dance religion saw meaning in this coincidence, a testimony for the power and credence of Wovoka's vision.

While calling for peaceful relations with non-Indians in the present world, Wovoka did not mention non-Indians in his prophecy, and many inferred that they were not to be included in the world to come. The date for fulfillment of the prophecy changed several times, after each successive date came and went uneventfully. The 1890 massacre, by troops of the U.S. Army, of Lakota (formerly called Sioux) who had gathered at Wounded Knee, South Dakota, for a Ghost Dance performance delivered a powerful message to other adherents of the religion.[1] In the end Wovoka called for the abandonment of Ghost Dance performances.

Wovoka's vision for the goals of the 1890 Ghost Dance religion as well as the means to achieve them were strongly influenced by his Northern Paiute heritage. Northern Paiutes and other Native people of the Great Basin (the geographic bowl bounded by the Sierra Nevada on the west and the Rocky Mountains on the east) share a worldview, which includes a belief in, and concept of, power. Every object in nature, animate or inanimate, has power: animals, mountains, rocks, caves, springs, lakes, lightning. Humans are part of the natural environment and can tap into this world of power. Power from the natural world manifests itself as a spirit who appears to the person in a dream or vision. Some people are passive recipients of power from a guardian spirit (for example, an animal); others actively seek it by going to a special place in nature associated with power, perhaps a mountain or a spring. Wovoka's visionary experience in heaven and God's revelation to him of the Ghost Dance religion followed a validated tradition for gaining sacred power.

Often, the communication and transfer of power from the natural world to people is through, or as, song. Wovoka's claim of having received the power to control weather from God followed this convention. He stated that he had five songs, each with discrete powers, "the first of which brings on a mist or cloud, the second a snowfall, the third a shower, and the fourth a hard rain or storm, while when he sings the fifth song the weather again becomes clear" (Mooney 1896: 773). The notion that Ghost Dance song and dance had the power to affect the natural world and human health—even resurrecting the dead—is only a variant of a myriad of other examples that appear in Great Basin mythology. For example, a Northern Paiute myth describes the creation of the moon as follows: "Then the Whippoorwill who had a fine voice and was a wonderful enchanter sang one of his magical songs and danced one of his magical dances, whirling and eddying about the frog who stood in the center and who was slowly and wonderfully transformed into a moon. And when the Whippoorwill ceased his song he waved his head for the moon to depart and it ascended to the heavens, rolled swiftly through the sky directly over their heads, a bright beautiful full moon" (Powell 1971: 221).

Other communicated elements in the transfer of power include words and instructions, and sometimes dance—which was the case of the Ghost Dance in Wovoka's vision. Power from nature given in dream inheres in the waking human performance of song, dance, and words. The correct realization of these three empowered and empowering elements influences the natural world: health, plant and animal food sources, and weather.

Wovoka drew not only on Great Basin notions of power but more specifically on the traditional Great Basin Round Dance and its religious associations.[2] As background for understanding this tradition, one must know that much of the land in the Great Basin is dry and food resources relatively scarce. In the past Great Basin people moved about in small family groups in order to exploit the natural resources. Only at the time of pine nut harvests or communal rabbit hunts was there enough food to support larger gatherings. It was on these special occasions that people performed the Round Dance, an ancient tradition in the Great Basin. Like the Ghost Dance, the Round Dance lasted five days, used the same dance formation and step, and had the same musical form in its songs, which the dancers sang without any instrumental accompaniment. The Round Dance was largely a social occasion, but at the same time it provided an opportunity for expressions of religious intent and meaning. There were prayers for health, fertility of plants and animals, and rain. However, beyond these spoken prayers, the dance itself, the songs, and their song texts and their communal performance all had power, working in concert together. Wovoka's predictions for a new earth and resurrection of the dead, even his songs for rain, can be seen as extensions of the religious goals of the Round Dance and its means for achieving them.

Wovoka's vision for the Ghost Dance combined his own Northern Paiute background, both the Round Dance tradition as well as an earlier 1870 Ghost Dance religion, with a variety of cultural contacts. In 1935 Leslie Spier suggested other Indian influences besides those of the Great Basin contributed to Wovoka's conception of the Ghost Dance. He noted the similarities between the Ghost Dance religion and earlier religious and prophetic traditions from Native people of the interior plateau area in the Northwest. Spier mentions other possible influences from Indian prophets, such as Smohalla, and syncretic Indian religions, such as the Shakers.

Wovoka also drew on Christian influences, which he learned while living with a non-Indian Presbyterian family during his youth. Along with other family members he listened to nightly readings from the Bible. It is significant that in his vision Wovoka received power not from an eagle or some other creature in the natural world but from God in heaven, two Christian terms and concepts. He again referred to God as the source of his weather songs. Similarly, Wovoka's predictions for earthquakes and other cataclysmic events that were to presage the destruction of this world when the new world arrived and the dead returned also suggest familiarity with Christian apocalyptic images for the end of the world and Judgment Day. Finally, scholars such as James Mooney (1896), Garold D. Barney (1986), and Michael Hittman (1990) have discussed from a variety of points of view the question of Mormon influence on the religion.

The 1890 Ghost Dance religion has traditionally been understood as a single homogeneous entity. However, my own recent work with the Wind River Shoshones of Wyoming leads me to a different conclusion. I believe that there were, in fact, two distinct branches of the Ghost Dance religion: a Great Basin branch, to which the Northern Paiute and Shoshones belong, and a larger Plains branch.

By rights, Wind River Shoshones could have belonged to either branch of the Ghost Dance. If you visit them today in Wyoming, you will see much evidence of their history from the eighteenth and nineteenth centuries, when they were a Plains people—hunters of the bison and warriors competing for hunting grounds. But interestingly, all of this is totally absent in their rendering of the Ghost Dance, which they performed until the late 1930s. The Shoshone Ghost Dance bears the imprint of their origins in the Great Basin and its enduring cultural legacy. Shoshones called the religion *Naraya*, which refers to the shuffling step of the dance. Emily Hill and Dorothy Tappay, two elderly Shoshone women, have taught me the meaning of the religion. According to Emily, "They say when you sing those songs it makes berries grow and makes grass grow, makes water run. Plenty of berries for in the fall, fish, everything. Sing for them, our elk and deer and all them. That's what it's for" (Vander 1988: 11). To sing of berries, grass, water, fish, elk, and deer was to help bring them and their abundance into being.

Emily described another major function of *Naraya* performance:

Well, some men, they dream that something's going to be wrong or some kind of sickness or some kind of storm. They know it. Well, we going to dance. It ain't going to happen when we dance. Flu or measles or scarlet fever or a sickness that's some kind of hard cough—one person knows when he's asleep, he knows it's coming. . . . We better be dancing, sending it back, sending it back. We just make it go back. That's the way they dance it. It isn't just a dance. . . . Well, it's a song for health. . . . When you don't feel good, when you feel sick or something, you dance with them. You feel good then. That's what it's for. It ain't just songs. (Vander 1988: 11–12)

There is no reference to Wovoka's Ghost Dance predictions in this explanation of the *Naraya*. However, resurrection of the dead and the coming new world do appear in a few of the *Naraya* songs that Emily and Dorothy sang and indicate that at some earlier time these beliefs were part of the *Naraya*. If there had been dates in the past for when these events were to occur, they had surely come and gone. I can only surmise that these predictions had been discredited in Emily's and Dorothy's eyes. But the remainder of the religion remained living faith for them throughout their lives. Nature—plants, animals, and water—and health lay at the heart of the *Naraya*. This was also true of the Great Basin Round Dance, which, as noted above, I believe to be the principal source of the *Naraya*. Wovoka's 1890 Ghost Dance doctrine overlaid the *Naraya*, adding its predictions for the return of the dead and destruction of this world at the advent of the pristine new world. After the demise of the Ghost Dance movement, this overlay eroded, but the ancient Shoshone core of the *Naraya* endured.

In contrast, other Plains tribes who had no cultural ties to the Great Basin took Wovoka's prophetic doctrines and elaborated them according to their own traditions and worldview. One can clearly see the sharp contrast between the Great Basin and Plains branches of the Ghost Dance in a comparison of their published song texts. People, often from the first-person perspective, appear in almost every Plains Ghost Dance song. People rarely appear in *Naraya* songs and are totally absent in published Northern Paiute songs. The difference, however, goes well beyond just the presence or absence of people. Plains Ghost Dance songs focus on a way of life: games, gambling, hunting buffalo, bow and arrows, and tepees, all harking back to the old nomadic Plains life, which by 1890 was finished. Nature itself played a relatively small part in these songs. On the other hand, in Shoshone *Naraya* songs (which constitute the largest sample of texts from the Great Basin branch), people and cultural references to everyday life are virtually absent. The majority of topics and images center on the natural world: miniature ecologies in which water in many forms, mountains, animals, green vegetation, and rocks are the central images. This is also true in all published Northern Paiute Ghost Dance texts.

The following two song texts, the first from a *Naraya* song and the second from a Lakota Ghost Dance song, illustrate the different orientation of the Great Basin and Plains Ghost Dance.

Young game animals, young game animals,
Young game animals, young game animals
On green mountains, green mountains *ena,*
On green mountains, green mountains *ena.*

In this text, *ena* is not a Shoshone word but a nonlexical syllable, or vocable, that serves as an ending marker.

Now they are about to chase the buffalo,
Now they are about to chase the buffalo.
Grandmother, give me back my bow,
Grandmother, give me back my bow.
The father says so, the father says so.
(Mooney 1896: 1070)

Mooney informs us that Wovoka, the Ghost Dance prophet, is the "father" in many Ghost Dance texts.

Both the Great Basin and Plains branches of the Ghost Dance religion were based on a belief in the creative power of Ghost Dance performance—whether it might be to bring about a new world and restore a former way of life or to ensure natural abundance in this world, prevent illness, and cure illness. Where do the Ghost Dance songs and their power come from? Emily Hill commented on the source of *Naraya* songs: "They dream it someplace way off, someplace in the mountains or hills someplace. Indians dream their songs. They dream it and they're going to sing it" (Vander 1988: 13). I have been told by other Shoshones that the dreamer learns the song after only one hearing—proof of its authenticity and power. Wovoka's claim to five powerful weather songs from God is a variant on the tradition of dreamed song. From Natalie Curtis we glimpse how the Lakota experienced it.

[Songs] . . . come in dreams or in visions through the spirits from *Wakan-Tanka* [literally, sacred-great (Powers 1975: 45) and translated elsewhere by Curtis as the Great Mystery]. . . . When the spirit comes to man in a dream, it may be thus: a song is heard on the air, then a form appears. This form is of a man, often dressed or painted in some particular or strange way. It is a spirit, who gives to the man a message, a teaching, or a song. When he turns to go, he takes, in disappearing, whatsoever form may be his own,—if he be animal, he will take the form of bear, buffalo, or bird—whatever his nature.
(Curtis 1923: 60, 61)

Mooney describes a different process for the generation of Ghost Dance songs by Plains tribes. He writes that it was after rather than during the vision that Ghost Dancers "embodied their visions in songs, which were sung . . . afterward in the dance, and from that time the Ghost Dance was naturalized in the south and developed rapidly along new lines. Each succeeding dance resulted in other visions and new songs, and from time to time other hypnotists arose, until almost every camp had its own" (1896: 899).

The powerful source, function, and meaning of Ghost Dance songs is all important to Shoshones and other Native American groups. Beyond some rare comments by Emily Hill, which indicated her special enjoyment of certain *Naraya* songs (Vander 1988: 16), I have never heard any Shoshone person discuss or analyze the aesthetics of *Naraya* songs. Indeed, I know of no published analysis of the aesthetics of Ghost Dance songs by any Native American person. By shifting my discussion at this point from the creative power of the Ghost Dance religion and its songs to the creative style of its music, my perspective, by necessity, also shifts—from Native American to Euro-American. There has been a scholarly tradition for studying Ghost Dance musical style, beginning with George Herzog in 1935, whose characterization has become the conventional understanding of the style. Privileged with an extensive repertoire of Ghost Dance recordings—something that Herzog did not have available to him—I want to build on his characterization, and at the same time redress omissions that I believe render it incomplete. My motive is to demonstrate the full range of aesthetic possibilities and achievement in these small and seemingly simple forms.

Ghost Dance songs, unlike their Great Basin and Plains texts, are surprisingly uniform. This is surprising, because the musical styles of the Great Basin and Plains are very different. Ghost Dance choreography and song form, which derived from the Great Basin, remained intact by all the groups who followed Wovoka's teachings. (My discussion of Ghost Dance musical style is based primarily on 147 *Naraya* songs, the largest corpus of recorded and transcribed Ghost Dance songs. Although *Naraya* texts are uniquely Shoshone in their Ghost Dance and Round Dance orientation and origins, their musical style is completely consistent with that heard on earlier Ghost Dance recordings and seen in musical transcriptions by James Mooney [1896], Frances Densmore [1929], and Natalie Curtis [1923].)

Herzog's 1935 study remains the fundamental starting point for understanding some of the most important characteristics of Ghost Dance musical style. "The melodic range is usually narrow, essentially a fifth. As a rule there is no accompaniment. Many of the phrases end on the tonic [for example, in the key of D, the final note is D]. They fall into sections so symmetrical as to be startling in primitive material. This

[margin handwritten note: chorus of song]

symmetry is achieved by the most essential feature of the style, a simple structural device: *every* phrase is rendered twice. The emphasis on 'every' is important . . . and is unique in Plains music" (403–4).

Musical examples 7.1, 7.2, and 7.3, two from the Plains and one from the Great Basin, exemplify Herzog's description of Ghost Dance style.[3]

Herzog's statistical study focused on a few musical elements—melodic range, phrase endings, and form—and demonstrated their shared common traits. His study justly points to the symmetry and simplicity of Ghost Dance songs. *Naraya* songs add further data that strengthen Herzog's characterization of Ghost Dance musical style. However, as I transcribed and studied the large sample of *Naraya* songs, I began to sense that there were many facets of the style that balanced its symmetry and simplicity in an opposing yet complementary manner. Because these songs are miniature forms, only microscopic attention to details can bring individual irregularities into view. I believe that summed together, their diversity and multitude are equally impressive. *Naraya* musical style embraces a host of asymmetrical and complex features within its simple symmetrical framework. A great wealth of examples and analyses of these matters appears in my previous publications (Vander 1986, 1997); however, the need for brevity here dictates that only a few examples be

Musical example 7.1. Lakota Ghost Dance song, *Wanagi Wacipi Olowan* III (Curtis 1923: 67).

Musical example 7.2. Lakota Ghost Dance song, *Wanagi Wacipi Olowan* II (Curtis 1923: 66).

presented. Other Ghost Dance songs share these same qualities with *Naraya* songs, and I shall point out instances in the musical examples 7.1, 7.2, and 7.3.

Repetition is central: not only is each song made up of a series of repeated phrases (*a a, b b,* and so forth), but the song itself was repeated many times while the dancers completed at least one revolution of the circle. Because the songs are brief, taking less than a minute to perform,

Musical example 7.3. Northern Paiute Ghost Dance song
(Vennum 1986: 704 [recorded by T. T. Waterman, 1910]).

many repetitions would have been necessary to accomplish this. Working against or as complements to repetition are the following elements: variation from inexact repetition, asymmetry from an unequal balancing of parts, contrasting musical elements, and interrelationships between the different paired phrases that obscure their separateness.

There is a continuum for all the many forms of inexact repetition that one finds in *Naraya* songs in general, which apply to *Naraya* song 1 in particular (musical example 7.4). For example, compare the first notes of both A sections: D in the first, and E in the second. Small variants of this magnitude are common. Within very narrow limits, they are interchangeable alternates that occur during song performance. In some cases, however, the variation is greater—for example, the setting of *So-go-vi* (Earth Mother) in sections B[1] and B[2]. The first setting of the word begins on the beat. Its syncopated rhythm shifts -*go* and -*vi* onto the second half of the beat. The second setting begins on an upbeat, and as a consequence -*go* and -*vi* fall on the beat.

Unlike the smallest example of inexact repetition in the A section,

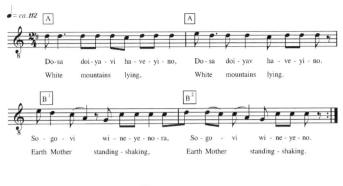

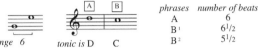

Musical example 7.4. *Naraya* song 1. Transcribed by Judith Vander. Emily: "Snowy mountains, white mountains. . . . It means spreading all over the world—where it's snowing" (Vander 1986: 43). Water in all of its forms (and one of the objects of *Naraya* performance) was the most common image in *Naraya* texts. Mooney wrote that mention of the snowy earth in a Northern Paiute Ghost Dance text may possibly refer to the new earth of Ghost Dance prophecy (1896: 1054). At some earlier time this may have been equally true for *Naraya* song 1.

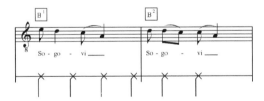

Musical example 7.5. Excerpts of *Naraya* song 1. Transcribed by Judith Vander.

the difference between the two B sections is of a greater magnitude. The two variant settings of *So-go-vi* appear in every repetition of the song and always in the same order. Therefore, my label for the two sections is B¹ and B² (see musical example 7.5).

One also finds inexact repetition in the Ghost Dance song given in musical example 7.1. In 1923 Curtis published her transcription of a Lakota Ghost Dance song to which Herzog later added letter labels for the different sections of the song, and also to 7.2. He judged that the different starting note in each A section (E in the first, F sharp in the second) was long enough or important enough to justify labeling the sections, A¹ and A². The Northern Paiute Ghost Dance song given in musical example 7.3 reveals a host of other types of inexact repetition. The largest point of irregularity is, in fact, the lack of repetition of both sections of the song: A repeats, but B does not. Sections A and B are themselves made of two repeated subdivisions; however, in section A, the second subdivision is a shortened version of the first and ends on E, the note above the tonic, rather than the tonic, D. The two halves of the B section have the same music, but their texts differ. The text for the second half of B comes from section A and foreshadows the return to the A section.

Besides inexact repetition, another source of irregularity in *Naraya* songs arises from an unequal balance between its parts. For example, different sections of a song have different lengths: section A in example 7.4 has six beats, section B¹ has six-and-a-half beats, and section B² has five-and-a-half beats. This lack of uniformity is the rule, and one sees it in Ghost Dance examples 7.1, 7.2, and 7.3 and in *Naraya* examples 7.4, 7.6, and 7.7. (Each song transcription is followed by a listing of the number of beats used in each section of the song.)

The use of contrasting musical elements is another source of complexity in *Naraya* songs, and the contrast may be of many kinds. For example, notice that in section A of musical example 7.6, the underlying rhythmic organization is based on groups of two and multiples of two; section B is based on groups of three and multiples of three. Or the contrast may be between different tonal centers. In musical example 7.4, D is a strong focal point and final note in section A; C is equally strong in B¹ and B² and is the final note of both B sections. One might argue that there are two different tonal centers for each different section. Another contrast may be between two different types of melody, one that is active and undulating (covering more ground) and another that is more static and straight-lined (reiterating a note or oscillating between two neighboring notes). In both musical examples 7.4 and 7.6, more static melodies in the A sections contrast with the more active melodies in the B sections.

Another type of contrast appears in musical example 7.7 and has to do with the setting of the text to music. In Ghost Dance songs, every note of music usually carries a new syllable of text. In Example 7.7, this is true in section A, but notice the places in section B where one syllable carries over and glides down from one note to the next (indicated in the transcription by slur marks over the notes). Such exceptions to the usual text-setting rule stand out and represent another type of unequal balancing. The Lakota Ghost Dance song given in musical example 7.1 shows similar exceptions to the customary one-to-one correspondence

Musical example 7.6. *Naraya* song 2. Transcribed by Judith Vander.
Emily: "They're wild ducks, little baby ducks, going along following
each other. They're swimming in the good water" (Vander 1988: 20).
(See song 5 in Vander 1988.)

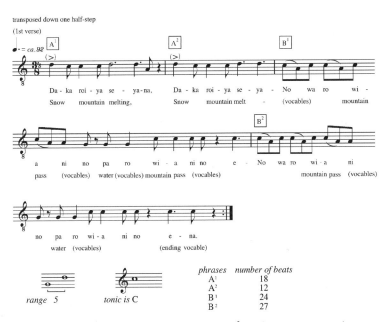

Musical example 7.7. *Naraya* song 3. Emily: "Snowy mountains,
melting. You know, when the sun's on the mountains, you see that
snow shining . . . when it's kind of going to melt" (Vander 1986:
43–44).

of text to music (also indicated in the transcription by slur marks over the notes).

Finally, a host of musical and textual relationships between the sections in *Naraya* songs are major contributors to their overall asymmetry and complexity. In number and variety, they seem infinite. Example 7.8 is a case in point.

This small text has two repeated lines, each in turn made of two subdivisions. Every line and subdivision begins with the same word, *mugua* (soul). Parallel musical settings match the parallel texts. They all begin on a note that then moves to a repeated higher note (see musical example 7.9).

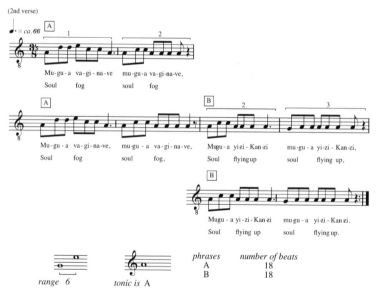

Musical example 7.8. *Naraya* song 4. Emily: "The soul is like a fog when it gets out of the body. Well, when a person dies, the soul goes out of the body and flies in the air" (Vander 1988: 25). (See song 10 in Vander 1988.) Fog is an important image in *Naraya* songs—being one form of water—and often envisioned on the mountains. It is also the Shoshone conception for the soul when it leaves the body after death. Notice that *fog* is the only meaningful word that appears in musical example 7.3, a Northern Paiute Ghost Dance song. Northern Paiutes also conceive of the soul in the form of fog, and for this reason it had special resonance in Ghost Dance texts. Wovoka told his converts that Jesus and all the dead who were already on the earth and returning to life appeared as "clouds."

Musical example 7.9. Excerpts of *Naraya* song 4. Transcribed by Judith Vander.

Musical example 7.10. Excerpts of *Naraya* song 4. Transcribed by Judith Vander.

Two of these settings, which appear in different sections of the song, are identical. In fact, all the music in the second half of A is identical to all the music in the first half of B (see musical example 7.10).

The placement of these two identical subsections within the entire form of the song results in an interesting integration of its parts. In musical example 7.8, I have added brackets and numbers in my transcription to identify every subdivision of the song. Using these numbers, the abstract patterning of the song is as follows:

A   A   B   B
1   2   1   2   2   3   2   3

The only place where the identical halves of sections A and B come together is in the center of the song. Sitting on either side of the division between the two lines, the side-by-side placement of the same music tends to obscure the boundary point. What had been an ending in A now becomes a beginning in B.

Finally, the parallel musical settings for *mugua* (soul) given in musical example 7.9 reveal another type of progression that moves throughout the song and all of its repeated sections. In every setting the melody moves from a starting note to repeated higher notes; however, the distance between them consistently decreases. At first they are four notes apart, then three, and then two. A further subtlety to this pattern is that every setting begins on A, the tonic note, except for the last one (circled in the transcription), which begins on G, a second below the tonic. This is another example of musical contrast and its spare, asymmetrical use.

To reiterate and summarize, a union of all the qualities in *Naraya* and other Ghost Dance songs contributes to their creative musical style and artistic achievement. Variation from inexact repetition, asymmetry from an unequal balancing of parts, contrasting musical elements, and complex relationships between different sections all complement the fundamental symmetry of its paired form. From this union emerges a style that is, by turns, simple and subtle.

Is there a relationship between the power of Ghost Dance songs discussed in the first half of this chapter and the aesthetic qualities described in the second half? For me, this remains an unanswered, perhaps unanswerable, question. All I can say is that from the perspectives of both Native Americans and Euro-American music scholars, Ghost Dance songs are intensely creative: the first perceives their sacred power to shape events in the natural world, and the second perceives their aesthetic power to shape a distinctive form of poetry and song.

Acknowledgment

I gratefully acknowledge that this work was made possible through the support of a research grant and fellowship from the National Endowment for the Humanities.

Appendix: Note on Orthography

a	as in f*a*ther
e	as in p*a*y
ë	as in *a*bove
i	as in el*i*te
ï	as in s*i*t
o	as in n*o*
u	as in l*u*te
ü	as in p*u*t
oi	as in n*oi*se

Key to Musical Transcriptions

 3's / **8**   ♪ = one beat, underlying rhythmic organization of threes (or multiples thereof) but not invariable, and with no implied bar line or accent pattern

 2's / **4**   ♩ = one beat, underlying rhythmic organization of twos (or multiples thereof) but not invariable, and with no implied bar line or accent pattern

 Slurs indicate that a word, syllable, or vocable sustains through the music until the next word, syllable, or vocable appears

e - vïn

 Marks the end of a musical section

 Marks a subdivision within a musical section

(>) Slight accent

A, B Sections of a song

A¹, A² Standardized variant forms of a musical section

Notes

1. The term *Sioux* is considered derogatory by Native Americans. Historically, scholars have used it to refer to three groups, the Lakota, Dakota, and Nakota, or Yankton. Mooney's study of the Ghost Dance and the publication by him and other scholars of Sioux Ghost Dance songs are, in fact, references to the Lakota (William Powers 1996, personal communication).

2. Although earlier scholars, such as James Mooney (1896), Robert Lowie (1909), Leslie Spier (1935), and Willard Z. Park (1941), have made statements that connect the 1890 Ghost Dance with the Great Basin Round Dance, and more recently Michael Hittman (1973) has connected the 1870 Ghost Dance with the Great Basin Round Dance, all of these scholars have lacked extensive data to develop this connection. Privileged with a large body of new data, I have been able to develop this relationship in a detailed way (Vander 1997).

3. In musical example 7.3, I have reformatted Thomas Vennum's transcription in order to bring out my analysis of the form of this song. Sectional subdivisions do not always coincide with the bar lines. In all other regards, this is an exact copy of Vennum's transcription, including the 4/4 meter marking. Vennum informs me that he perceives each beat to be subdivided into triplets (1996, personal communication). Because it would be easier to play or sing this transcription if the meter marking were 12/8 rather than 4/4, I have added a 12/8 meter in brackets after the 4/4 meter of the original.

References

Barney, Garold D. 1986. *Mormons, Indians, and the Ghost Dance Religion of 1890*. Lanham, Md.: University Press of America.

Curtis, Natalie. 1923. *The Indians' Book*. Reprint, New York: Dover Publications, 1968.

Densmore, Frances. 1929. *Pawnee Music*. Reprint, New York: Da Capo, 1972.

Herzog, George. 1935. "Plains Ghost Dance and Great Basin Music." *American Anthropologist* 37: 403–19.

Hittman, Michael. 1973. "The 1870 Ghost Dance at the Walker River Reservation: A Reconstruction." *Ethnohistory* 20: 247–78.

———. 1990. *Wovoka and the Ghost Dance.* Carson City, Nev.: Grace Dangberg Foundation.

Lowie, Robert H. 1909. "The Northern Shoshone." *Anthropological Papers of the American Museum of Natural History* 2:165–306.

Mooney, James. 1896. *The Ghost-Dance Religion and the Sioux Outbreak of 1890.* Reprint, Lincoln: University of Nebraska Press, 1991.

Park, Willard Z. 1941. "Cultural Succession in the Great Basin." In *Language, Culture, and Personality: Essays in Memory of Edward Sapir,* edited by Leslie Spier, A. I. Hallowell, and Stanley S. Newman, 180–203. Menasha, Wisc.: Sapir Memorial Publication Fund.

Powell, John Wesley. 1971. *Anthropology of the Numa: John Wesley Powell's Manuscripts on the Numic Peoples of Western North America, 1868–1880,* edited by Don D. Fowler and Catherine S. Fowler. Smithsonian Contributions to Anthropology 14. Washington, D.C.: Smithsonian Institution.

Powers, William K. 1975. *Oglala Religion.* Lincoln: University of Nebraska Press.

Spier, Leslie. 1935. "The Prophet Dance of the Northwest and Its Derivatives: The Source of the Ghost Dance." *American Anthropological Association General Series in Anthropology* 1.

Vander, Judith. 1986. *Ghost Dance Songs and Religion of a Wind River Shoshone Woman.* Monograph Series in Ethnomusicology no. 4. Los Angeles: University of California.

———. 1988. *Songprints: The Musical Experience of Five Shoshone Women.* Urbana: University of Illinois Press.

———. 1997. *Shoshone Ghost Dance Religion: Poetry Songs and Great Basin Context.* Urbana: University of Illinois Press.

Discography

A Cry from the Earth: Music of the North American Indians. Folkways Records, FC 7777.

American Indian Soundchief: Pawnee 600. Soundchief.

American Indian Soundchief: Ponca 600. Soundchief.

Great Basin: Paiute, Washo, Ute, Bannock, Shoshone. Library of Congress, AAFS L38.

Kiowa. Library of Congress, AAFS L40.

Plains: Comanche, Cheyenne, Kiowa, Caddo Wichita, Pawnee. Library of Congress, AFS L39.

Sioux. Library of Congress, AFS L40.

Shoshone, accompanying cassette tape for *Songprints: The Musical Experience of Five Shoshone Women* (*Naraya,* songs 2 and 4 in this chapter, appear in *Songprints* as numbers 5 and 10, respectively, and are included on the accompanying cassette tape.)

Songs of the Pawnee and Northern Ute. Library of Congress, AFS L25.

Sound of Indian America: Plains and Southwest. Indian House, 9501.

8 An Acoustic Geography of Intertribal Pow-wow Songs

TARA BROWNER

At modern-day intertribal pow-wows, there are two distinctive regional singing styles commonly referred to by participants and observers as "Northern" and "Southern." Of the two, Southern singing, the conventional style of Oklahoma, is the most similar to the traditional performance practices of Omaha/Ponca *Heluska* songs—the songs ancestral in some way to almost modern pow-wow songs because of their influences on formal song structure. Northern style, having been strongly influenced by Warrior Society songs of the northern plains and Great Lakes regions, predominates from the midplains northward, and its performance locales include the territories surrounding the Great Lakes and Pacific Northwest. In areas where pow-wows have been more recently established, such as the American Southwest and the American and Canadian northeastern woodlands, pow-wow musicians have a tendency to sing in styles not native to their geographic setting, and often adopt the pow-wow singing style closest in sound (that is, range and vocal production) to their own traditional tribal repertories. For example, Navajo singers, who are geographically located in the Southwest, tend to sing Northern style because vocally it is closer to their traditional songs than Southern style. Pueblo singers, who live in the same general area as Navajo, usually prefer singing Southern, which in range and vocal production technique is similar to their ceremonial repertory.

Since the 1950s, a number of factors, including urban relocations and accessibility to recording technologies, have resulted in a series of musical alterations in both Northern and Southern styles that go far beyond basic formal structures, and represent shifts at a deeper aesthetic level as to what sounds "good" to both singers and their audiences. But more important, certain genres within the pow-wow repertory have taken on new meanings beyond the event itself. Key among these is the development of the generic intertribal pow-wow song, those medium-tempo multipurpose songs with texts entirely of vocables that accompany rounds of intertribal dancing. As these songs are traded from group to group, recorded during live performance, and turned into the core repertories of urban Drums with multitribal memberships, the obvious question arises concerning whether intertribal songs maintain any sense of connection to their original cultural and tribal source.

In order to understand the origins of intertribal songs and how they differ musically from each other, a new taxonomy of pow-wow song making is necessary, one that examines the music more rigorously than the simple binary of Northern and Southern, but less specifically than the level of individual tribal cultures. Due to their lack of Native language texts and relatively generalized sets of vocables, intertribal songs allow for musical assessment based almost entirely on melodic traits, ornamentation, and vocal-production techniques rather than through the usual linguistic, historic, and larger formal comparative elements such as song structure. Because we can assume that the latter three characteristics will be similar, analysis can be concentrated more on nuanced aural signifiers such as vocal timbre, tempo, phrase structure, and the rhythmic counterpoint created by vocal stresses playing off against the main melody. Pow-wow musicians and dancers (some participants act in both roles) discern musical origins through a variety of ways, but most of all people simply listen to a song, plugging it into an aesthetic framework that is more than intuitive but less than systematic. It is this level of analysis that I intend to explore in this essay, using intertribal songs as the mode of inquiry.

Historical Perspectives

The separation of Northern and Southern repertories was probably an essential fact in the earliest spread of the Omaha/Heluska/Grass Dance musical form, which has been documented by Clark Wissler (1916) and his informants as beginning in the 1830s. The "Omaha" Dance was in all likelihood a musical form as much as a Warrior Society, and the form, which included an internal repetition and energetic beat pattern with stresses on the second beat of each grouping, proved popular among tribes from the mid-1800s onward. To think that the Omaha Society completely displaced existing Warrior Societies is to assume that tribes did not value their own traditions, and it is far more plausible that Omaha Dancing was grafted on to indigenous Warrior Society ceremonials as it spread across the plains. This is especially true in the Great Lakes region, where the Omaha Society never fully took hold, even though the formal structure of its music did.

From the earliest days of intertribal pow-wows (beginning around 1880), the proximity of Oklahoma tribes to one another contributed to an overarching "Southern" pow-wow musical aesthetic in the old Indian Territory, and the "traditional" sound of Oklahoma singing has changed relatively little since the late 1800s. It was far different, however, in the North. Northern tribes are spread over a far greater land area, and as settlers gradually took up the newly unoccupied lands between reservations, Northern Indian nations not only became geographically separated from one another but also experienced a kind of musical isolation from the Southerners as well. Bureau of Indian Affairs policies controlling travel between reservations also inadvertently fostered a climate of musical diversity, limiting cross-fertilization, and led to the splitting off of Northern from Southern styles by the early 1920s, especially in regards to musical form. Orin Hatton has outlined four general historic periods of Northern Omaha song performance (Hatton uses the term *Grass Dance*)—development and diffusion (1840–90), common practice (1890–1920), Northern (1920–45), and regional (1945–70)—and suggests that the early 1970s mark the beginning of a fifth period (1986: 202–3). Although dancers from various tribes both Northern and Southern interacted in the Wild West shows of the 1880s–1920, and changes in dance styles unquestionably resulted from those contacts, a kind of aesthetic paradox also emerged in Oklahoma. In the old Indian Territory, modification and transformation in pow-wow *dance* style—specifically in the regalia and footwork of Fancy Dances—was far more acceptable than messing with the sound and form of the music.

Some Song-Form Basics

Before proceeding into more nuanced arguments, some basic information about contemporary pow-wow music is in order. Table 8.1 shows a series of music and dance categories in both Northern and Southern styles.[1] Categories are numbered I–V, and although songs can sometimes shift type *within* each category, they cannot jump from one category to another because the drumbeat patterns are too different. For example, it is possible that a "Traditional" song (one with Native language text) meant for Grass Dancers could have the text changed and eventually transform into a Women's Traditional Dance song, but it could *never* become a Crow Hop.

Table 8.1. Dance and music categories

	Northern	Southern
I	Flag Songs Crow-Hop Songs Snake Dance Songs	Flag Songs Horse Trot Songs Horse Stealing Songs
II	Traditional Songs Straight Songs Intertribal Songs Jingle Dance Songs a. Shuffle b. Round c. Two-Step	Fast War Dance Songs Slow War Dance Songs (for Straight Dancers)
III	Round Dance Songs Two-Step Songs Owl Dance Songs "49" Songs	War Mother Songs Soldier Dance Songs Round Dance Songs 49/War Journey Songs Two-Step Songs Scalp Dances
IV	Sneak-Up Songs	Buffalo Dance Songs

In characteristic performances of Northern and Southern pow-wow songs, short repetitive phrases with Native language texts (known as "word" songs) or vocables (known as "straight" or "intertribal" songs) are broken up by formulaic cadential patterns sung entirely in vocables, and are the core elements of modern pow-wow songs.[2] The only major overall change in performance practice after 1900 was the moving of the Honor Beats (also called "hard beats") to an internal position within Northern songs during the 1920s (Isaacs 1959: 108). This placement of drum accents, with Southern hard beats at the end of the second phrase, and Northern Honor Beats within it, is a key difference between Northern and Southern styles. Most pow-wow music is strophic (in verses) with an interior repetition, and each strophe is called a "round" (or "push-up") in Indian performance terminology. Figure 8.1 illustrates and contrasts Northern and Southern musical forms. Old style Northern Crow Hop songs, however, can sometimes be made up of a single verse with no interior repetition, which is just repeated over and over again. These songs, along with a few others that occasionally pop up at pow-wows, are remnants of pre-Omaha/Grass Dance musical forms.

Many of the old Lakota Grass Dance songs recorded between 1915 and 1917 by Frances Densmore are purely in vocables, and vocables do not intrinsically possess patterned rhythms (see Densmore 1918). Repetitious Native language texts, however, are much more inclined toward fixed rhythmical patterns, suggesting that the texted portions of a song

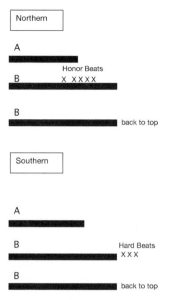

Figure 8.1. Northern and
Southern song forms.

are "made" (composed) first, and the rest of the song proceeds from them. At a later date, as performance traditions changed and vocables subsumed texts, the practice of repeated rhythmically identical phrases remained. With tribal-specific cadential patterns already in place, making an entire song was (and is) as simple as coming up with one short melodic phrase, setting it to vocables, adding appropriate cadences, and plugging it into the appropriate form. Within the form, however, there are unlimited possibilities for variation, including phrase length, tempo, drum accents, vocal embellishments, melodic contour, and overall range.

Song categories for pow-wow music are fluid, with many songs serving dual purposes depending on the context of their performance. Songs originally made for Northern Men's Traditional dancers can easily be adjusted for Grass Dance competitions simply by slowing them down a bit, or might even work for Women's Traditional dancers if the tempo is further reduced and the text changed from Native language into pure vocables. From there, it is a quick jump from a Lakota "straight" song to a Navajo intertribal one if a Navajo with a handheld tape recorder is nearby, and then perhaps on to an urban drum group who hears it at a Phoenix pow-wow. Musical purists might find this process offensive, and more than one drum has been confiscated for singing a song belonging to another family, or even worse one that has been "put away." But from the standpoint of thinking about the songs outside of their cultural context, what really is the difference between a hypothetical Lakota straight song, its "borrowed" Navajo intertribal interpretation, and its new urban incarnation?

Current Song Terminologies: Indian and Academic

Since 1990, Native singers have developed new terminologies to deal with the processes of musical change, and explain how a tribal-specific "straight" version of a song differs from an "intertribal" performance of that same song by a Drum without roots in a single tribal culture. The expression usually used is "contemporary," and it describes a generic mode of performance outside of tribal or regional customs. "Contemporary" was first coined on the pow-wow circuit a little less than two decades ago, and describes a movement by many Northern urban Drums (and Drums that sing in the Northern style) toward a sound that is higher pitched than the older forms of singing, less heterophonic, almost devoid of tribal-specific vocal embellishments, and often lacking indigenous language texts. Songs in the contemporary style are almost always made up either entirely of vocables or of simple four- to five-word text phrases that can be pronounced by those outside the originating tribe (or those with limited Native language skills). Singers tend to pronounce the text exactly and synchronize their vocal delivery, avoiding the heterophony so characteristic of traditional Northern singing.

In contrast, "Original," also a Northern style, currently signifies reservation Drums with members from the same community or geographic area. These singers typically learn their songs from other tribal members and have some fluency in their Native language, and most began singing using what is commonly called the "Indian throat" at a young age (the Indian throat is a high chest voice, and for a man to do it well, he must start practicing this type of vocal production in his preteen years, before his voice breaks). Original singers are comfortable with heterophony and a more improvisational musical structure, and sing in tribal or regional styles.

When writing about pow-wow music, it is relatively easy to describe general song forms, and the differences between Northern and Southern modes of singing in the "Original" tradition. Texts about tribal specific repertories are also common, most recently by Luke Lassiter (Kiowa) (1998), Severt Young Bear and R. D. Theisz (Lakota) (1994), William Powers (Lakota) (1980, 1990), Bruno Nettl (Blackfeet) (1954), Judith Vander (Shoshone) (1988), and Thomas Vennum (Ojibwe) (1980). A recent book by Clyde Ellis (2003) deals specifically with Southern pow-wows (although more with history than music), and my own text, *Heartbeat of the People* (2002), looks at Northern music in a broader fashion, comparing Great Lakes and Lakota performance styles. But what's missing in this catalog is a sense of music in regional styles, that is, what happens *within* the Northern and Southern geographic areas. These are difficult comparisons to make and lines to draw, but through my years of dancing with a "Western ear," I have come to recognize regional styles that exist inside of the larger geographic areas traditionally delineated by the terms *Northern* and *Southern*. And the easiest way to parse these regional styles out is by listening to intertribal songs, in which the hearer does not have Native language texts to worry about. In addition, listening to music as purely evocative rather than analyzing its performance theoretically allows for finer distinctions in sound quality, and perhaps a richer vocabulary when describing how it sounds, as opposed to just how it is structured.

Hearing Pow-wow Music

Figure 8.2 illustrates my own personal taxonomy of pow-wow singing, and how I hear regional style when I listen and dance to the music. Interestingly enough, for me, urban Drums are often characterized by the *absence* of style, especially when I hear an intertribal song. Below is a generalized listing of musical traits I use when listening comparatively in order to distinguish regional or tribal origins of intertribal songs. It is personalized in the way that every person hears music differently, but nevertheless gives a sense of how songs that in a surface sense might seem similar actually *sound* different from region to region.

Sound Characteristics: Southern

Southern Prairie: Low, rich male voice, natural singing without vocal tension. Higher female voice, slightly nasal. Heavily accented high pitches provide a rhythmic counterpoint to the drum part.

Southern Plains: Low voice, slight vocal tension, transparent in quality. Female voice also tense. High pitches are stressed, but not enough to give a counterrhythm to the drum part. Melodies often modulate up a whole step after the first round.

Sound Characteristics: Northern

Great Lakes: Medium-high voice, often with a gravelly or rough timbre. Melodic structure is often in five-beat phrases. Women's part high and tense.

Midplains: Medium-high voice, somewhat tense, parts sung loosely and often in heterophony. Ornamentation of melody is common, and

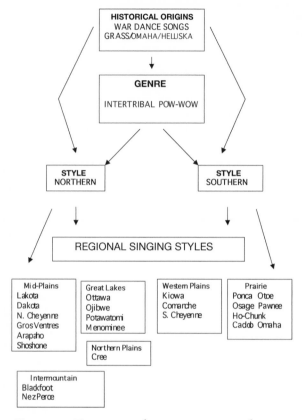

Figure 8.2. Taxonomy of pow-wow song styles.

ornaments are stereotyped. Women's part is tense and nasal. Northern Arapaho melodies can include microtones, generally flat minor thirds. Lakota songs often increase in tempo after the first round.

Northern Plains: High male voice, very tense and rhythmic. Female voice nasal and sirenlike. Melodies jagged with short phrases and empty spaces with no vocal lines.

Intermountain: High male voice (females often sing male part), voice tense but not strident. Blackfoot songs often increase in tempo at the end of the second round, and cadential patterns are microtonal, with a "quivering" sound of a flat half-step.

Some Conclusions

Pow-wow music is in an ongoing state of sonic transformation, due in large part to the forces and pressures of competition, commodification, and migration from tribal homelands to urban areas (and the return of these people to their reservations). But what I find most remarkable is the shift in the purpose of the music, from complementing dancing ("accompanying" would be a misnomer) to existing on its own as a genre of popular music, listened to purely for the pleasure of its sound alone. And the closest analogue to pop music is the intertribal song as interpreted by urban Drums in the "contemporary" style. Although I doubt that intertribal songs fulfill the same role in Native people's lives as country-and-western songs, it has become obvious over my years of traveling the pow-wow circuit that for many participants, intertribal songs (as well as tribal-specific ones) fill a specific sonic and emotional void, especially when speeding down a rural highway played at full blast on the car stereo. Detached from their original function and meaning, the songs create a kind of portable Indian space, not really an extension of the pow-wow arena but instead an intensification of self. But in order to study the songs and parse their origin, rate of musical change, and codification in the new contemporary style, scholars must first recognize the existence of regional styles within the larger geographic divisions of Northern and Southern musical areas.

Notes

1. This list is not meant to be exhaustive, and covers the basics at most urban pow-wows. Different regions each have their own preferred repertory of songs, and a "Traditional" song in the Great Lakes region is often called a "War Dance" song farther West. Also, whereas in many areas the term *Grass Dance* refers to a style of dancing, in the Northern Plains it can also mean musical style and is synonymous with the "Omaha" musical style. In Oklahoma, however, Omaha Dances are essentially the *Heluska* Dances done by the Poncas, and the Northern "Omaha" songs do not closely resemble the Ponca *Heluska* songs in vocal style or range.

2. *Straight* is the Northern term to describe a song where the text is made up exclusively of vocables, but straight songs generally are considered tribal-specific. *Intertribal* is an expression used in both Northern- and Southern-style areas to describe songs—also with texts solely—that are sung to accompany rounds of intertribal dancing. It is the latter type of song that is the focus of this article.

References and Selected Bibliography

Black Bear, Ben, Sr., and R. D. Theisz. 1976. *Songs and Dances of the Lakota.* Aberdeen, S.D.: North Plains Press.

Browner, Tara. 2002. *Heartbeat of the People: Music and Dance of the Northern Pow-wow.* Urbana: University of Illinois Press.

Densmore, Frances. 1918. *Teton Sioux Music.* Bureau of American Ethnology Bulletin 61. Washington, D.C.: Smithsonian Institution.

———. 1951. *Songs of the Sioux.* Washington, D.C.: Library of Congress, AAFS L23.

Ellis, Clyde. 2003. *A Dancing People: Powwow Culture on the Southern Plains.* Lawrence: University Press of Kansas.

Hatton, Orin. 1986. "In the Tradition: Grass Dance Musical Style and Female Pow-wow Singers." *Ethnomusicology* 30, no. 2: 197–221.

Howard, James. 1983. "Pan-Indianism in Native American Music and Dance." *Ethnomusicology* 28, no. 1: 71–82.

Isaacs, Tony. 1959. "Oklahoma Singing." *American Indian Hobbyist* 5, no. 9: 106–10.

Lassiter, Luke E. 1998. *The Power of Kiowa Song: A Collaborative Ethnography.* Tucson: University of Arizona Press.

Nettl, Bruno. 1954. *North American Indian Musical Styles.* Philadelphia: American Folklore Society.

Powers, William. 1980. "Oglala Song Terminology." In *Selected Reports on Ethnomusicology,* 3, no. 2, edited by Charlotte Heth, 23–41. Los Angeles: Program in Ethnomusicology, University of California–Los Angeles.

———. 1990. *War Dance: Plains Indian Musical Performance.* Tucson: University of Arizona Press.

Vander, Judith. 1988. *Songprints: The Musical Experience of Five Shoshone Women.* Urbana: University of Illinois Press.

Vennum, Thomas. 1980. "A History of Ojibwe Song Form." In *Selected Reports on Ethnomusicology* 3, no. 2, edited by Charlotte Heth, 43–73. Los Angeles: Program in Ethnomusicology, University of California–Los Angeles.

———. 1982. *The Ojibwa Dance Drum: Its History and Construction.* Washington, D.C.: Smithsonian Institution Press.

———. 1989. *Ojibway Music from Minnesota: Continuity and Change.* St. Paul: Minnesota Historical Society.

Wissler, Clark. 1912. "Societies and Ceremonial Associations of the Oglala Division of the Teton-Dakota." *Anthropological Papers of the American Museum of Natural History* 11, no. 1: 3–99.

———. 1916. "General Discussion of Shamanistic and Dancing Societies." *Anthropological Papers of the American Museum of Natural History* 11, no. 12: 853–76.

Young Bear, Severt, and R. D. Theisz. 1994. *Standing in the Light: A Lakota Way of Seeing.* Lincoln: University of Nebraska Press.

9 | Singing Indian Country

DAVID W. SAMUELS

Country Music and Ethnic Boundary Crossing

In the song "Indian Cowboy," Midnite Ethelbah, lead singer of the band Apache Spirit, delivers one of the more famous lines in contemporary Native American country music: "I don't know how it happened, but I'm feeling kind of glad / I'm an Indian cowboy, and being both can't be so bad."[1] The rhythm of the couplet's second line is perfectly timed to coincide with the chorus's V-I, E-to-A musical resolution, along with the bass line that walks up to the signature guitar riff that frames each of the song's verses. It is the kind of seamless blending of country-and-western form and Native American content that has made Apache Spirit a Native American Music Award–winning band, among the best-known performers of contemporary Native American music today.

How can this be? By what magical process can Anglo-American country music come to sonically represent Indians as well? How can the sounds of white, hardscrabble, blue-collar, evangelical Christian, sometimes racist ideologies be embraced by the very people against whom those ideologies have often been so destructively employed? For anyone who has ever seen a western movie where the Indians are brought to crushing devastation in order to make room for the cowboys and their cattle, the musical image must be jarring in spite of—or perhaps because of—its presentation of stylistic concord. What episode of *The Twilight Zone* is this? How can Indians sing cowboy music? Are they for real?

These obvious and undeniable contradictions may lead some people to dismiss Indian country singing as hopelessly assimilated. How can any self-respecting Native American get pleasure from these musical sounds so closely associated with the usurpers of their culture and history? Are they Indians at all, or are they just out of their minds?

I have caricatured them a bit, but these are the kinds of questions I hear from students, especially teaching in the Northeast, where an "eclectic" global taste in music is often further specified as "I listen to everything but country." But the relationship between cowboys and Indians has always been complicated. Neither the cowboy nor the Indian can escape a history of media representations—from Buffalo Bill's Wild West shows to Washington-versus-Dallas football games—that have caricatured them and placed them side by side on the same stage. Neither are these images limited to the sideshows of "least-common-denominator" entertainments. Chic "Southwest-style" fashion performs a similar task, using more sophisticated means. One high-end western lifestyle magazine calls itself *Cowboys and Indians*, and features ads for designer fashion boots and silver jewelry, as well as columns on building "your Western and Native American art collection." As Michael Martin Murphey sings in his song "Cherokee Fiddle," "Now the Indians are dressing up like cowboys / And the cowboys are putting leather and turquoise on."

Despite country music's associations with white working-class lifeways, country performers as well sometimes trade on the possibility of a Native American heritage. Hank Williams claimed to be part Creek and Cherokee, and has been inducted into the Native American Music Hall of Fame, as has Crystal Gayle (Cherokee). Ten years ago, Canadian country star Shania Twain caused some controversy when she supposedly claimed that she was part Ojibwa.[2] And for years Johnny Cash allowed rumors of his supposed Cherokee heritage to circulate in the media, finally coming clean in a 1975 interview with Larry Linderman, who asked, "A number of press reports have stated you're part Cherokee. Are you?" Cash replied, "No, I have no Indian ancestry. Some folks have said I do, but I can't find it anywhere—and I've got my family tree. Of course, when I used to get high, well, the higher I got, the more Indian blood I thought I had in me. And a lot of people wanted me to be part Indian, especially after I recorded the *Bitter Tears* album" (Streissguth 2002: 153).[3]

Cash's mentioning his 1964 *Bitter Tears* recording, a collection of songs shedding much-needed light on a number of Native American political issues, raises another set of complications about country music. The genre is so closely associated with working-class southern white aesthetics in the minds of many listeners—accurately or not (see Ivey 1998, Malone 1985, and Peterson 1997 on the mixture of blues and country in the early twentieth century, and the commercial decisions that led to a separation of "race" and "hillbilly" genre categories in the marketing of recorded music)—that it is difficult to imagine anyone *other* than working-class whites deriving any pleasure or meaning from the sounds of the music. Timothy D. Taylor (2007) has observed that *Bitter Tears* is the *only* country recording included in the two-volume *Rough Guide to World Music*. This absence not only flies in the face of dozens of Native American country performers who sing their lives through its musical conventions but also reveals how marginalized the sounds of country music can be in the ears of even sophisticated and open-minded listeners. This silence has often included professional ethnomusicologists, a topic I will return to in a later section.

Given this multiplicity of contexts and crossings, when it comes to Indian country singing, asking, "How can this be?" is an alienating question. It treats the subject of the question as something completely beyond the possible experience of the person asking. Yet it may be that we all have experiences of loving deeply music that is arguably beyond our cultural experience—Renaissance madrigals, Balkan gangas, Motown, salsa, sitars, swing. Why are Native Americans singled out as needing to resist these same circulating influences in order to convince non-Indians that they are who they claim to be? The question about Indians and country music is not simply about the anomalies of that particular combination. Those anomalies are read through dominant historical ideologies about what a proper expression of Native identity should be.

And so we might instead turn to another question that is at the heart of a great deal of contemporary Native American musical expression. Despite increasing concern for, involvement in, and resurgence of musical practices that can be claimed as "traditional," a core question about contemporary Native American musical practice in cultural context today is, "What counts as culture?" In this chapter I want to explore some possibilities for thinking about country music as an important way that Native American songwriters and performers give voice to contemporary issues of indigenous culture, history, and identity. I have divided the chapter into two broad sections. In the first, I will discuss the historical and cultural forces that have created a context for Native country performers. In the second, I will explore some of the musical and textual processes by which Native performers make country music meaningful within that historical and cultural context.

Country Music as a "Genre"

In beginning to grapple with the relationship of country music to the voicing of these historical and political concerns, we immediately come up against a crucial feature of contemporary Native American music making:

Native performers are extremely eclectic in their sources and influences. In his work on contemporary music in indigenous communities around the world, Martin Stokes has written of these eclectic stylistic choices: "Musicians in many parts of the world have a magpie attitude towards genres, picked up, transformed and reinterpreted in their own terms" (1994: 16). This means that few Native country singers perform in the country genre exclusively. Like country music itself, their styles reveal influences from across the southern swath of the West, extending from Tennessee and Kentucky to Louisiana and California—rhythm and blues, Louisiana "swamp pop" (Bernard 1996), Texas swing, and Mexican border polkas. Like Johnny Cash, Waylon Jennings, Tammy Wynette, Elvis Presley, Loretta Lynn, Roy Orbison, Tanya Tucker, Conway Twitty, or Buddy Holly, they owe as much to rock-and-roll as they do country-and-western. When I did my fieldwork on the San Carlos Apache Reservation, I learned that a number of country performers were inspired to learn guitar by California surf music, especially by the release of the play-along album *Play Guitar with the Ventures* (1965). And a great many country performers were influenced by such country-rock hybrid crossover bands of the '60s and '70s as the Byrds and the Eagles.

This generic eclecticism is combined with a varying embrace of the key generic markers of country singing. A love of country music among Native performers and songwriters does not automatically mean that the defining features of country music are simply copied verbatim. For example, many Native country singers do not fully appropriate all aspects of country music vocal style in their performances. Only a few singers, for instance, incorporate the sonic features of the Appalachian, Ozark, and mountain South dialect of American English into their pronunciations when they sing, despite the importance of the sounds of that vocal style to the performance of mainstream country (Feld et al. 2004). The Fenders, one of the earliest country groups from the Navajo Nation, at times sang heartfelt renditions of country songs without a hint of any save their own local Navajo-English dialects. Similarly, very few bands incorporate fiddles or pedal steel guitars into their instrumental textures.

And so we have to recognize a variety of legacies, as well as varying commitments to unreservedly embrace a country music aesthetic. This means that the relationship between Native country singers and country music is by no means simple. There are many layers and levels of engagement with country music displayed by Indian country singers. Listening to a political activist such as Floyd Red Crow Westerman singing "Custer Died for Your Sins" or "They Didn't Listen" to the accompaniment of a pedal steel guitar, it is tempting to think that this must all be ironic—that an Indian must sing country with tongue firmly in cheek. And there is that. But irony is not the only way in which Native Americans are politically and creatively engaged with the sounds and forms of country music. Although the Fenders do not perform the sonic markers of white "redneck" southernness in their singing voices, this is not completely a matter of ironic detachment from country music. The members of WigWam, a country band from northern Ontario, compose and sing all their songs in their native language, Anishinabe. The group's full-on country arrangements and style act as the musical bed for these songs of cultural history and identity. The late Buddy Red Bow adopted a fluent country style to sing about Lakota history, culture, and hard times on the Pine Ridge Reservation, often blending his compositions with an array of New Age sounds and excerpts of Pow-wow Grass dance songs as well. In this wide variety of artistic engagements with country style, rarely is the "purity" of the country music genre at stake—if such a thing exists to begin with.

Rethinking Our Questions

What, then, *is* at stake? Taking note of the abundance of style mixing in contemporary Native American country music, we might rethink the kinds of questions we ask about it. "Why" questions can be asked in ways that imply different kinds of underlying questions. The sense that there is a contradiction at work here is strong, and so the "why" question is sometimes taken to mean, "How could Indians possibly sing country songs? How could this be?" *That* version of the question asks us only to focus on the sense of contradiction involved. It puts the pieces that make up Native American country music at irreconcilable odds with each other, and then wonders how these jigsaw puzzle pieces could ever have been thought to fit together. But there is another version of the question that can encourage us to think about how contradiction produces expressive artistry.[4]

The first version of the question offers little way out, and can lead to frustration. One way of resolving that frustration has been for people to hold onto the idea that it is the Indian things that are added to a country song—native instruments, native vocables, native vocal styles—that make it Native, as if a real Indian couldn't simply love a mainstream hard-country artist (Ching 2003) like Merle Haggard, George Jones, or Hank Williams and mean it. But my experience on the San Carlos Apache Reservation contradicts this. Everyone I knew on the San Carlos reservation knew and loved hard-country standards such as Merle Haggard's "Branded Man" and George Jones's "Open Pit Mine," and could sing them by heart. I once heard an entire audience sing Haggard's "Silver Wings" in unison as the band played it. One man in San Carlos mused that if there were a collection of Johnny Horton's greatest hits, every adult on the reservation would own a copy.[5] And the great Canadian country singer Ernest Monias has recorded a sixteen-song album, *Tribute to Hank Williams*. Moreover, as I noted earlier, Hank Williams is in the Native American Music Hall of Fame.

The Locations of Musical Meaning

Finding the "meaning" of a song amid this array of artistic influences, debts, and crossings is daunting. We will not be able to locate the entirety of a song's meaning within the "song itself"—certainly not within the most popular commercial recording of a song. Rather, we must think about the dynamic relationship between songs, performers, and audiences as a necessary feature of musical meaning—or any meaning taken in its sense of a fully social, cultural production (Duranti and Brenneis 1986). It is something of a truism to say that artists do not control the meanings that audiences will take away from their work. But truism or not, this will be a key to making sense of what is initially striking as the contradiction of American Indian country singing.

The productive engagement of the audience in the creation of social meaning is crucial to understanding contemporary cultural expression. It may be even more central in the case of a musical style such as country, which has depended so heavily on the technologies of mass mediation—especially radio and records—for the spread of its popularity (Jensen 1998; Peterson 1997). Although the notion of performer-audience relations is commonplace when one thinks about live performances, it may seem like a bit of an anomaly to consider the audience when discussing mass-mediated music heard on radio and records. But the response to mediated performances involves the social imagination precisely because they are linked to private, individual, and social responses to experiences of music. Boe Titla, a singer-songwriter on the San Carlos reservation, told me that when he was in high school, he and his friends would rush home every afternoon to listen to the thirty minutes of country music broadcast by a local station in Safford, Arizona. Many people in Boe's hometown of Bylas owned battery-operated transistor radios to listen to music even before their homes were wired for electricity. Those high school days were when Boe fell under the spell of George Jones. When Boe began writing his own songs about important places and events in the history of the San Carlos Apache people, he said they came out naturally in what he called "that George Jones style" (Samuels 2004: 168).

Stories like Boe's show us that, even in the case of mediated performance, we cannot assume that we understand musical meaning without exploring the active participation of audience members in producing meanings from their musical experiences. Roland Barthes alludes to this in literature through what he calls "readerly" texts, in which "the reader [is] no longer a consumer, but a producer of the text" (1974: 4). Charles Keil and Steven Feld have developed an anthropology of culturally grounded musical meaning through their concept of "participation consciousness" (Keil and Feld 1994). Through this social aesthetic of communication, musical form is something that is experienced by its various "coparticipants"—a term that potentially erases the false dichotomy between "performer" and "audience." Tara Browner's discussion of the concentric circles of a pow-wow, with the drum at the center, makes an analogous point—especially her discussion of George Martin's conceptualization of the space, in which the division between "performers" and "audience" is overcome by having all participants located within the outer circle of "a final protective layer of spirits" (2002: 98).

What Does the Country Voice Accomplish?

To understand why participating in country music is so powerful for so many Native Americans, we need to shift slightly the way we ask questions about the supposed immutable meanings of country music. Rather than wonder why in the sense of "how is this possible?" we might ask it in the sense of "what does it accomplish?" In that latter sense we can ask, "What kinds of participation and expression does the *choice* of country music style make possible for Native people? What can one say in a country style that might be different from what one can say, for example, within the musical frameworks of rock, reggae, or hip-hop?"

First, the country music voice is a premier means of expressing thoughts and feelings about attachments to the past—the sense that events in the past refuse to recede into the past, and continue to influence one's everyday life in important ways. I will explore this in greater detail below, but you can sense it in album titles such as Red Blaze's *Memories and Daydreams*, and in Norman Beaver's voice when he sings in Anishinabe, "I'm thinking back every day as it really happened . . . the truth I'm searching, the past I'm reaching," in the title song of WigWam's *Adisokaan*. Second, country songs often highlight the alienation of urban life, and a preference for older, more rustic, rural ways (Fox 1996). In the song "Quiet Desperation," Floyd Westerman longs for the "smell of sweetgrass on the plain." Similarly, Buddy Red Bow and Winston Wuttunee use the aesthetics of country to sing about their boyhood memories.

Country Music in the Literature on
American Indian Music

I want to turn now to the passing relationship that ethnomusicology has had with Native country singers. Though Indian country music has sometimes played an important role in the writings of anthropologists and ethnomusicologists, country music may, in fact, play a less prominent role in the musical life of Native American communities today than genres such as rock, hip-hop, and gospel. The Native American Music Awards combine "country" and "folk" into a single category—and it has been some time since a country band or performer has actually won the category.

The notice taken of country artists by scholars of music and culture may also be due to these writers' focus on rural or reservation communities rather than urban communities, as well as the importance of the West, and in particular the Southwest, in the history of ethnomusicology after World War II. The creation of undergraduate textbooks also played a part. David McAllester's inclusion of the Fenders' version of Johnny Cash's "Folsom Prison Blues" on the audio cassettes or compact discs that supplement the undergraduate textbook *Worlds of Music* (Titon 1984)—and the subsequent inclusion of that recording in the audio supplement to John Kaemmer's textbook *Music in Human Life* (1993)—accounts in part for the prominence of Native American country music in academic circles.

There is a well-worn joke about every Navajo family consisting of a mother, father, two children, and an anthropologist, and the fascination with the Pueblos of New Mexico and Arizona for anthropologists and ethnomusicologists extends back into the nineteenth century. Given these long-standing affinities and proximities, one could assume that these scholars were well placed to notice when Navajo and Zuni started playing country music. For many years, however, ethnomusicologists found it difficult to write about Native American popular music at all, let alone country music, except insofar as it registered cultural disintegration.

There is a thread that we can follow, however, to give us some sense of how scholars thinking about music and culture developed an approach to these kinds of musical practices. In 1952 Willard Rhodes wrote of the survival of traditional Native American music as demonstrating that Western, European, or American culture had had very little influence on Native musical styles and practices. He concluded that this in turn demonstrated the truth of Curt Sachs's cultural-historical assertion that change in musical style occurred more slowly than changes in other cultural domains such as food preparation or transportation—that music is one of the most robust of cultural artifacts, remaining consistent to itself in spite of sometimes massive changes to other aspects of a culture.

A decade later, however, Rhodes (1963) wrote about 49s—"Indian melodies with English words," he called them. In that article, Rhodes noted that these songs had a history dating back to "Wild West" shows and other theatrical performances that toured the world in the late nineteenth century. This observation challenged his earlier assertions about tenacious stability. It also pointed to a seventy-five-year gap in ethnomusicologists' engagement with the relationship among music, language, culture, and the politics of ethnic identity.

Rhodes referred to these songs as "hybrid music." I believe that his may be the earliest use of the concept of "hybridity" in this sense. For Rhodes, these songs were an "index of acculturation," a way of measuring the extent to which Euro-American society had corrupted, or at least influenced, Native American cultural practices. In the early 1970s another ethnomusicologist, George List (1971), offered another way of thinking about these changes, observing that these new songs were usually arch jibes at the moon-June-swoon proclivities of American popular love-song composers. List thus opened up the possibility—as we discussed earlier—that ironic detachment was an important mode of Native engagement with Bureau-American cultural domination.

David P. McAllester, most widely known for his classic treatments of Navajo ceremonial practices, included a discussion of the Fenders in his article on music for the Southwest volume of the *Handbook of Native American Indians* (McAllester and Mitchell 1983).[6] Recent years have seen increased interest in writing about contemporary musical practices in Native American communities. A special issue of the journal *World of Music* was dedicated to the topic (Neuenfeldt 2002).

If country music has been underrepresented in the scholarly literature, the same cannot be said of its place in the work of contemporary Native American writers. Sherman Alexie (1994, 1996, 2001), Joy Harjo (1983), and James Welch (1991, 2001) in their poetry and fiction, and, for example, Craig Womack (1997) in his academic writing, have all used the conflicted image of the Indian cowboy and country music in order to portray the perplexities of disenfranchisement and connectedness at work in the formation of contemporary Native American identity. Alexie has perhaps been the most overt in this regard. In his story "The Toughest Indian in the World," the narrator compares country music legends (and lesser lights) to the world of Christian iconography: "It seemed that every Indian knew all the lyrics to every Hank Williams song ever recorded. Hank was our Jesus, Patsy Cline was our Virgin Mary, and Freddy Fender, George Jones, Conway Twitty, Loretta Lynn, Tammy Wynette, Charley

Pride, Ronnie Milsap, Tanya Tucker, Marty Robbins, Johnny Horton, Donna Fargo, and Charlie Rich were our disciples" (2001: 23). Canadian scholars have written more extensively about Native American country singing than have their peers below the border (Whidden 1984; Witmer 1973, 1974).

Country Music and Cultural Assimilation

Music has been an important part of the assimilationist practices of Bureau-American religious, government, and educational institutions in Indian country since the beginning of the reservation era, if not earlier.[7] Music was an important way of monitoring the social practices of Indian communities. Not only the things incarcerated Native people sang about—was rebellion afoot?—but the way they did things in groups was important (Feld 1988). Singing in unison and harmony was not just seen as aesthetically pleasing in comparison to Native ways of vocalizing together but was further associated with the inculcation of democracy, modernity, and Christianity in Native communities. Hymn singing, in either English or Native languages, was taught and encouraged. Many mission and government boarding schools featured bands, and a number of elders on the San Carlos reservation have an undying love of John Philip Sousa's marches as a result of having performed in these bands as schoolchildren. These new practices not only were coded as "white" and "Christian" in opposition to "red" and "pagan" but also carried heavy implications of middle-class cultural values and the prestige associated with mastery of those practices. Zitkala-Sa studied violin at the New England Conservatory of Music and collaborated with William Hanson in composing an opera, *Sun Dance*. Musical training was an important aspect of both church and school programs. On the San Carlos reservation, the Lutheran missionary's sister gave piano lessons, and a number of people who spoke with me had taken some.

These new musical practices were certainly not accepted unthinkingly. For one thing, the official policies of churches, educators, and government agencies, as well as the ways in which they were carried out by local representatives, were neither monolithic nor absent any internal inconsistencies. For example, there was a great deal of debate over whether education should be bilingual or in English only (Spack 2002), a debate that had repercussions for the composition of and singing of hymns. The possibility of a successful policy of complete assimilation is further complicated by the presence of a number of highly trained Native American teachers, such as Zitkala-Sa and Luther Standing Bear, who bore witness to the continuing importance of Native lifeways. The notion of the inculcation of "white" cultural values was also complicated by the use of African American educational institutions, such as the Hampton Institute in Virginia, as sites of Native American instruction.

At the same time, local communities had their own means of interpreting the cultural meanings of musical practices. For example, the piano was a highly gendered musical instrument on the San Carlos reservation, considered a feminized means of making music. One man told me that he was teased by his friends for taking up the piano, because it was seen as something "for girls." The piano was also a highly salient marker of middle-class status in the United States (Parakilas 1999), and very few Apaches could afford the expense of having a piano in the home.

Beyond the raced, cultured, classed, religioned, and gendered contact points of school and church, other forces were also at work, forces that were more masculine, popular, and commercial. The man who remembered being teased for playing the piano also recalled purchasing a guitar through the Sears catalog. On that guitar, he and his brother learned American cowboy songs and Mexican ranchera numbers. Partly for this reason, country music has tended to be a masculine domain, although this certainly has not excluded women from singing it. A number of women usually categorized as "folk," such as Cherokee Rose, Sharon Burch, Joanne Shenandoah, and of course Buffy Sainte-Marie, have wafted over to country styles occasionally, and certainly in the last instance might even be considered country artists by some listeners.

The introduction of radios onto the San Carlos reservation also brought access to music from distant places into the community. Like many across the United States, people in San Carlos would tune into Grand Ole Opry broadcasts. But according to many people I have spoken with, the genre of music was not all that important. People would tune into stations from Winkelman, Safford, and Globe, "just looking for good music," as Boe Titla said (Samuels 2004: 136). Here we return to the question of the "purity" of genre in the context of contemporary Native musical practices. Genre mixing among country, pop, rock-and-roll, and Mexican music was prevalent. The Rice school would occasionally hold sock hops—where, according to my consultants, only the girls would dance, the boys standing outside and looking on.

Out of this amalgam of forces and histories emerged the first bands of the 1950s and 1960s—the Fenders, the Navajo Sundowners, the Zuni Midniters, the Isleta Poorboys, Apache Spirit. In those bands, country music lived side by side with Mexican, surf, and rock. On the San Carlos Apache Reservation, as in many other Native American communities, most bands played a mix of styles and genres.

Musical Processes in Native American Country

Having looked at the social histories that came together to form country bands in Native communities in the mid-twentieth century, let us now consider some of the musical processes of composition and performance that transform country music into a powerful medium for the voicing of various Native American identities. I wish to consider five main aspects of these musical practices: "cover" versions of country hits by Native performers, the use of country expression and aesthetics to forge connections to a sense of homeland and place, country music as a way of creating connection to social history, the creation of country songs with Native-language texts, and the production of "hybrid" musical performances that blend the soundscape of country music with that of traditional Native musical practices.

The first thing to consider is the role of "cover" versions of country hits by Native bands and singers. It is easy to think that this is the least "Indian" and therefore the most problematic aspect of contemporary country performance in Native American communities. Hearing El Coochise singing "Tulsa Time," or listening to the Sioux Savages or the Navajo Sundowners singing "Rainy Day Woman," one might dismiss it as assimilation in its rawest form. This judgment assumes a fairly simple relationship between Waylon Jennings, the members of the Sundowners, and the wider Native American musical community. But the relationship is actually fairly complicated, with a number of different intervening mediations between singer and listener. These layers of mediation include the mediating technologies of production (songwriter, microphone, producer, engineer), as well as the technologies of distribution (radio, recording, audiotape, compact disc), all of which play a part in the relationship between Waylon Jennings's singing voice and the response it evokes in his various audiences. This is why the relationship between mainstream recording artists and their consuming and listening audiences is so crucial. The Sundowners are one among a number of *intermediators* who make Waylon Jennings a performer with local Navajo meanings. We return, here, to the social processes of participation through which forms of political and cultural domination are creatively engaged. If many people on the San Carlos reservation were exposed to country music by sitting in front of a radio after school, they were also exposed to it through listening to recordings of Indian country bands. One San Carlos singer I spoke with told me that his mother ordered so many Fenders records from up in Navajo country that for a while he thought she was having an affair with a Navajo (Samuels 2004: 109).

Waylon Jennings probably was not thinking of Native American groups like the Navajo Sundowners when he wrote and sang "Rainy Day Woman." But the Sundowners played a key role in making the song Native American. Often, when I asked people on the San Carlos reservation who originally sang one country song or another, the response I got was not "Merle Haggard" or "Waylon Jennings" or some other Nashville star. It was "the Fenders," "the Sundowners," "the Midniters." Among the most important of these cover versions are "Rainy Day Woman," "Sweet Dream Woman," "Wine," "T for Texas," "Driving My Life Away," "Same Old Tale," "Folsom Prison Blues," "Branded Man," and "Silver Wings."

A second process that links country music to Native American ideologies of culture and history is the sense of connection to land and place. As country music is thoroughly emplaced in the rural, the rustic, and the hardscrabble, its global circulation has often involved the way it allows indigenous communities to sing of land, place, and memory (Fox forthcoming). Red Blaze uses country sensibility for the evocation of attachment and memory—the line "long-gone memories keep on buggin' me," in their song "Chains of Change," simultaneously evokes a country and Native stance on the place of memory and the past in contemporary life. The Zuni Midniters' use of an easy triplet feel country-rock setting to sing their political protest "You took my land / You made it your country" is in that sense a logical choice.[8] Country music links the personal to the political through sung narratives of loss (Fox 1992, 1996). Boe Titla uses this resonance to the fullest in his original compositions about places and histories of the San Carlos Apaches. Similarly, Buddy Red Bow, J. Hubert Francis, Floyd Red Crow Westerman, and Edmund Bull use the sensibilities of country music to sing of the feeling of, and for, place.

Another closely related feature linking country sensibility and Native American ideology is the turn toward the past as a way of deeply experiencing one's self-knowledge. A sense of historical connectedness pervades the lyrical texts of Native country songs. Boe Titla's songs about the places that are important to the San Carlos Apaches evoke social histories because the importance of those places is strongly attached to the stories of the things that happened in those places (Basso 1996). These songs evoke an emotional attachment to place by linking feelings for historical events to feelings for musical form. Boe credits the mood evoked by his songs to the "George Jones style" of his songwriting. By mentioning a place, like Chiricahua Mountain or Point of Pines, in a song, Boe evokes memories in his listeners. And he is highly conscious of the idea that music can make you remember people and events. Boe does not account for these memories simply by pointing to his lyrics. Rather, it is the entire sung vocalization and instrumental arrangement that he talks about: "Maybe the *sound* that I put in there, the *mood*, the *emotion* of the song, or the *speed* of the song, or the *words* that touch them, that makes them see somebody, or back to those days, or something like that" (Samuels 2004: 169). In this quote, "words" are actually the last thing that Boe mentions. He places questions of timbre, emotion, and tempo first—all of which are features of country music's generic conventions for arousing affective responses.

Famous historical events and Native leaders—Sitting Bull, Red Cloud, Geronimo, Navajo Code Talkers—are also celebrated and remembered through country songs. A number of Canadian performers have made songs that commemorate the importance of the 1885 Northwest Rebellion, an armed confrontation led by the Cree chiefs Big Bear and Poundmaker, and the French Canadian champion of the Métis, Louis Riel.

A fourth process that transforms country music into a Native expression is found in the composition of country songs with Native language texts. These performers combine the feeling of country music, the importance of place and of historical memory, in texts that evoke indigenous identity by claiming particular linguistic territory as a meeting place of Native and non-Native identities and affective responses. WigWam sings of history, heritage, and land in their native Anishinabe language. Leonard Adam, born in Uranium City in northern Saskatchewan, sings country songs in his native Dene about memories of elders and being prepared to bear knowledge of culture and history into the future. Apache Spirit has composed and sung songs in Western Apache, such as "Nii Shi Chia Zhoo"[9] (You are beautiful to me) on *The Lawman,* and the liner notes of their second album, *Keep Movin' On,* are written in Apache.

Finally, there are hybrid processes at work in songs that incorporate Native styles of vocalization and Native instruments into the production of their country-and-western songs. On the song "Drum," Red Blaze mixes country with northern grass dance singing to proclaim, "Our way of life ain't gone forever." Apache Spirit often mixes the calls and bells of the *Gahn* into their songs.[10] Many country performers blend indigenous flutes and drums into their arrangements. And many more use Native vocable formulas, or incorporate Native songs into their vocal arrangements. The Red Bull singers appear as special backup vocalists on Edmund Bull's *Indian Boy.* Eagle Feather and Buddy Red Bow also have songs that bring traditional singers, usually songs associated with the northern pow-wow, into the mix as a means of staking claims of Native identity.

What Are These Voices Doing?

To return to our original reformulation of the central question about country singing: what does the country voice accomplish for its Native American singers? More than anything, country is the sound of memory, of the desire for days and places that are always both within and out of reach. If the rock voice is about rebellion, the reggae voice about protest, and the hip-hop voice about preaching truth, then the country voice is about memory. Country music is an important way for Native Americans to link social memory and sociopolitical position. This is one reason that political activists such as Buddy Red Bow and Floyd Westerman have found in country singing a participatory genre that allows them to voice their concerns. Country engenders a personal and social affective response in its listeners that allows people to experience cultural history through the tone, mood, meter, rhyme scheme, and instrumentation of the songs, be they cover versions of "Swinging Doors," songs in Cree with twin fiddles and steel guitars (George Strait's version of "Pure Country"), or songs about the land with a northern drum singing Fancy Dance songs in the background.

In Sherman Alexie's story "What You Pawn I Will Redeem" (2003), the protagonist, Jackson Jackson, a homeless Spokane Indian, is trying to scrounge up enough money to buy his grandmother's pow-wow regalia from a Seattle pawnshop. Despondent, he wanders down to the wharf, where he sees three homeless Aleuts sitting on the same bench where he had seen them the day before. After sitting in silence for a long while, Jackson asks the Aleuts a question:

> I thought about my grandmother. I'd never seen her dance in her regalia. And, more than anything, I wished I'd seen her dance at a pow-wow.
> "Do you guys know any songs?" I asked the Aleuts.
> "I know all of Hank Williams," the elder Aleut said.
> "How about Indian songs?"
> "Hank Williams is Indian."
> "How about sacred songs?"
> "Hank Williams is sacred."
> "I'm talking about ceremonial songs. You know, religious ones. The songs you sing back home when you're wishing and hoping."
> "What are you wishing and hoping for?"
> "I'm wishing my grandmother was still alive."
> "Every song I know is about that."
> "Well, sing me as many as you can."
> The Aleuts sang their strange and beautiful songs. I listened. They

sang about my grandmother and about their grandmothers. They were lonesome for the cold and the snow. I was lonesome for everything. (176)

In this passage, Alexie links country music, memory, and cultural history to an affective sense of exploitation and desire. In contrast to the original notion that ethnic Indian identity and hardscrabble white identity were somehow at odds with each other, here we experience a point at which ethnicity and class overlap. Obviously, the histories of working-class whites and Native Americans are not identical, but their trajectories overlap in the feeling of expropriation and alienation that is the result of the kinds of historical relationships with bourgeois "civilizing" practices that prefer pianos to guitars (Samuels 2004: 101). Jackson Jackson cannot find redemption because he cannot redeem his grandmother's pawned regalia, even though it is in the pawnshop because it was stolen. Jackson is homeless, and although his homelessness is due to a reason that he keeps secret because "Indians have to work hard to keep secrets from hungry white folks," his homelessness places him in an economic or class as well as an ethnic and cultural position. His economic position threatens to make it impossible to reclaim the loss of his grandmother's regalia. Hank Williams sings of loss, and it is the kind of affective attachment to the lost object that Native Americans can identify with.

Notes

1. See the suggestions for further listening at the end of this article.

2. In 1991 she had changed her name from Eileen to Shania—reputedly the Ojibwa word for "I'm on my way." As it turned out, her adoptive father was Native, but she had no Indian "blood" to lay claim to. The arguments stirred by Shania's statements revisited old questions of "nature" and "nurture," and whether "blood" or "upbringing" is what makes you who you are (see Strong and Van Winkle 1996).

3. It is instructive to compare this 1975 statement by Cash with Tom Dearmore's 1969 profile of Cash for the *New York Times Sunday Magazine,* in which the author wrote, "Cash, who has the face and stature of his Cherokee forebears . . ." (Streissguth 2002: 100).

4. The classic statement of this position about art can be found in Max Horkeimer and Theodor Adorno's "Dialectic of Enlightenment," in which artistic greatness is found not in the complete resolution (identity) of elements, but in the incomplete struggle for resolution and its inevitable failure.

5. Of course such a collection exists: Sony, 40665.

6. McAllester also included an extended discussion of the rock band XIT, led by Navajo tribal member Tom Bee, but as this chapter is concerned with country music, I will not discuss that. Tom Bee is currently the president of Sound of America Records, one of the more successful Native music production companies in the United States.

7. John Gregory Bourke (1891) wrote of an organ grinder who traveled the Southwest unharmed because the Indians found him so entertaining.

8. It is difficult, of course, to make a blanket statement about the uses of country sensibility. Country music itself has a history of attachments and separations with other musical genres, and the genre mixing found in Native communities creates more complications. The Zuni Midniters' songs crossed these boundaries at a time when both the style and the subject matter of many country and rock songs covered overlapping domains.

9. As with many Apache speakers, the orthography for writing Apache has not been standardized. A more standard linguist's orthographic rendering of the song title would be "nii shich'i zhoo."

10. Gaan are mountain spirits.

References

Alexie, Sherman. 1994. *The Lone Ranger and Tonto Fistfight in Heaven.* New York: Perennial.

———. 1996. *Reservation Blues.* New York: Warner Books.

———. 2001. *The Toughest Indian in the World.* New York: Grove Press.

———. 2003. "What You Pawn I Will Redeem." *New Yorker,* April 21–28, 2003.

Barthes, Roland. 1974. *S/Z.* Translated by Richard Miller. New York: Hill and Wang.

Basso, Keith H. 1996. *Wisdom Sits in Places.* Albuquerque: University of New Mexico Press.

Bernard, Shane. 1996. *Swamp Pop: Cajun and Creole Rhythm and Blues.* Jackson: University Press of Mississippi.

Bourke, John G. 1891. *On the Border with Crook.* Reprint, Omaha: University of Nebraska Press, 2001.

Browner, Tara. 2002. *Heartbeat of the People: Music and Dance of the Northern Pow-wow.* Urbana: University of Illinois Press.

Ching, Barbara. 2003. *Wrong's What I Do Best: Hard Country Music and Contemporary Culture.* New York: Oxford University Press.

Duranti, Alessandro, and Donald Brenneis. 1986. "The Audience as Co-author." *Text* 6, no. 3.

Feld, Steven. 1988. "Aesthetics as Iconicity of Style (Uptown Title); or, (Downtown Title) 'Lift-Up-Over Sounding': Getting into the Kaluli Groove." Reprinted in *Music Grooves,* by Charles Keil and Steven Feld, 109–50. Chicago: University of Chicago Press, 1994.

Feld, Steven, Aaron Fox, Thomas Porcello, and David Samuels. 2004. "Vocal Anthropology: From the Language of Music to the Music of Voice." In *A Companion to Linguistic Anthropology,* edited by Alessandro Duranti, 321–46. New York: Blackwell.

Fox, Aaron. 1992. "The Jukebox of History: Narratives of Loss and Desire in the Discourse of Country Music." *Popular Music* 11, no. 1: 53–72.

———. 1996. "'Ain't It Funny How Time Slips Away?': Talk, Trash, and Technology in a Texas 'Redneck' Bar." In *Knowing Your Place: Rural Identity and Cultural Hierarchy,* edited by Barbara Ching, 105–30. New York: Routledge.

———. Forthcoming. Introduction to *Songs Out of Place,* edited by Aaron Fox and Christine Yano. Durham: Duke University Press.

Harjo, Joy. 1983. *She Had Some Horses*. New York: Thunder's Mouth Press.

Ivey, Bill. 1998. Liner notes to *From Where I Stand: The Black Experience in Country Music*. Warner Brothers/Reprise, 947428-2.

Jensen, Joli. 1998. *The Nashville Sound: Authenticity, Commercialization, and Country Music*. Nashville: Vanderbilt University Press.

Kaemmer, John. 1993. *Music in Human Life*. Austin: University of Texas Press.

Keil, Charles, and Steven Feld. 1994. *Music Grooves*. Chicago: University of Chicago Press.

List, George. 1971. "Song in Hopi Culture, Past and Present." *Yearbook of the International Folk Music Council* 3: 30–35.

Malone, Bill C. 1985. *Country Music USA*. Austin: University of Texas Press.

McAllester, David P., and Douglas F. Mitchell. 1983. "Navajo Music." In *Handbook of North American Indians*, edited by Alfonso Ortiz, ed., 10:605–23. Washington, D.C.: Smithsonian Institution Press.

Neuenfeldt, Karl. 2002. "Indigenous Popular Music in North America: Continuations and Innovations." *World of Music* 44, no. 1.

Parakilas, James, ed. 1999. *Piano Roles: Three Hundred Years of Life with the Piano*. New Haven: Yale University Press.

Peterson, Richard A. 1997. *Creating Country Music: Fabricating Authenticity*. Chicago: University of Chicago Press.

Rhodes, Willard. 1952. "Acculturation in North American Indian Music." In *International Congress of Americanists: Proceedings of the 19th Congress*, edited by Sol Tax, 127–32. New York: Cooper Square.

———. 1963. "North American Indian Music in Transition: A Study of Songs with English Words as an Index of Acculturation." *Journal of the International folk Music Council* 15: 9–14.

Samuels, David W. 2004. *Putting a Song on Top of It: Expression and Identity on the San Carlos Apache Reservation*. Tucson: University of Arizona Press.

Spack, Ruth. 2002. *America's Second Tongue: American Indian Education and the Ownership of English, 1860–1900*. Lincoln: University of Nebraska Press.

Stokes, Martin. 1994. *Ethnicity, Identity, and Music: The Musical Construction of Place*. Oxford: Berg.

Streissguth, Michael, ed. 2002. *Ring of Fire: The Johnny Cash Reader*. New York: Da Capo Press.

Strong, Pauline Turner, and Barrik Van Winkle. 1996. "'Indian Blood': Reflections on the Reckoning and Refiguring of Native North American Identity." *Cultural Anthropology* 11, no. 4: 547–76.

Taylor, Timothy D. 2007. "You Can Take 'Country' Out of the Country, but It Will Never Be 'World.'" In *Songs Out of Place*, edited by Aaron Fox and Christine Yano. Durham: Duke University Press.

Titon, Jeff. 1984. *Worlds of Music: An Introduction to the Music of the World's Peoples*. New York: Schirmer Books.

Welch, James. 1991. *The Indian Lawyer*. New York: Penguin Books.

———. 2001. *The Heartsong of Charging Elk*. New York: Anchor.

Whidden, Lynn. 1984. "'How Can You Dance to Beethoven?': Native People and Country Music." *Canadian University Music Review* 5: 87–103.

Witmer, Robert. 1973. "Recent Changes in the Musical Culture of the Blood Indians of Alberta, Canada." *Yearbook for Inter-American Research* 9: 64–94.

———. 1974. "'White' Music among the Blood Indians of Alberta." *Canadian Journal of Traditional Music*.

Womack, Craig. 1997. *As We Are Now: Mixblood Essays on Race and Identity.* Berkeley and Los Angeles: University of California Press.

Further Listening

Adam, Leonard. *Spirit Flies.* Turtle Island Music.
Apache Spirit. *Indian Cowboy.* Canyon Records.
———. *The Lawman.* AltaVista.
Bull, Edmund. *Indian Boy.* Turtle Island Music.
The Country Siders. *The Country Siders.* AltaVista.
Eagle Feather. *No Boundaries.* Sunshine Records.
The Fenders. *Introducing the Fenders.* Hammerhouse Productions.
———. *On Steel.* Hammerhouse Productions.
Fenders II. *Out in New Mexico.* AltaVista.
Francis, J. Hubert, and Eagle Feather. *Reverence.* Sunshine Records.
Gladstone, Jack. *Noble Heart.* Hawkstone.
Monias, Ernest. *A Tribute to Hank Williams.* Sunshine Records.
One Ninety One. *Just for Her.* AltaVista.
Red Blaze. *Memories and Daydreams.* Turtle Island Music.
Red Bow, Buddy. *Black Hills Dreamer.* Tatanka Records, 4102.
Sioux Savages. *Sioux Savages.* Dine Records.
Stillwater Band. *Suspicion.* AltaVista.
The Thunders. *Volume 1.* AltaVista.
Watchman, Henry. *Rocking Rebels/Navajo Sundowners/Oldies.* AltaVista.
Westerman, Floyd Red Crow. *Custer Died for Your Sins.*
———. *The Land Is Your Mother.*
WigWam. *Adisokaan.* Sunshine Records.
Wuttunee, Winston. *The Best of Winston Wuttunee.* Turtle Island Music, TIM 30040.
Zuni Midniters. *My Land.* Hammerhouse Productions.

Contributors

T. CHRISTOPHER APLIN is a musician, researcher, and writer from Oklahoma. He has a masters of music from the University of Oklahoma–Norman, where he focused on American Indian musical practice and independent rock and pop music making within the state as both a researcher and a performer. At present, he works with the *American Indian Culture and Research Journal* at the University of California–Los Angeles, where he is currently a Ph.D. candidate in ethnomusicology.

TARA BROWNER (Choctaw) is professor of ethnomusicology and American Indian studies at the University of California–Los Angeles. She is the author of *Heartbeat of the People: Music and Dance of the Northern Pow-wow* (University of Illinois Press, 2002), and has published in the journals *American Music, Journal of Musicological Research,* and *Ethnomusicology*. Professor Browner is active as a dancer in the Women's Southern Cloth style.

PAULA CONLON is associate professor of music at the University of Oklahoma. She has been studying First Nations music and dance in Canada since the early 1980s when she wrote her master's thesis on the Canadian Amerindian flute. In 1993, she earned a Ph.D. in musicology/ethnomusicology from the University of Montreal; her dissertation is a semiotic analysis of three hundred Inuit drum-dance songs under the guidance of Jean-Jacques Nattiez. Since moving to Oklahoma in 1996, Dr. Conlon has participated in and attended a large variety of Native American ceremonials and social dances, given lecture recitals on Native American flute in Oklahoma and surrounding states, and written a biography of noted Comanche flutist-artist Doc Tate Nevaquaya, forthcoming from the University of Oklahoma Press. At the University of Oklahoma School of Music, Professor Conlon teaches world music, Native American music, and ethnomusicology classes at both the graduate and the undergraduate levels.

DAVID E. DRAPER (Choctaw) received an interdisciplinary doctoral degree in music and anthropology from Tulane University. His primary research and subsequent publications have focused on Afro-American and North American Indian music and culture. After holding teaching positions at California State University–Bakersfield and the University of California–Los Angeles, he is currently on the faculty of Delgado College in New Orleans. His interest in folklore resulted in serving two terms on the Board of the American Folklife Center in the Library of Congress.

ELAINE KEILLOR has been a professor at Carleton University in Ottawa since 1977, lecturing on Canadian musics, baroque and classical periods, ethnomusicology, and piano literature. She introduced the first Canadian university course on Canadian aboriginal musical expressions and is grateful to many elders and teachers who have willingly shared their wisdom on this subject. Her publications include monographs on aspects of Canadian music and essays in various encyclopedias and books, including the *New Grove Dictionary of Music and Musicians, The Garland Encyclopedia of World Music,* and *Die Musik in Geschichte und Gegenwart.* In 2004 she received the Helmut Kallmann Prize for Distinguished Service to Canadian musical research and performance. She is the leader of the team producing the Web site on aboriginal music, Native Drums, found at http://nativedrums.ca/.

LUCY LAFFERTY (Dogrib Nation) was born near Hislop Lake, Northwest Territories. Lucy (Lisi in Dogrib) was surrounded with the singing of her parents about the land, its animals, and hearing stories from her grandparents. Before she was sent to spend ten months of the year at various residential schools beginning at the age of six, she had developed a keen appreciation of the songs used for Ti dances and for traditional Dogrib *(Tli Cho)* hand games. After completing her high school education, she became a teacher's assistant, and eventually a teacher, as she completed a bachelor of education degree at the University of Saskatchewan. Involved with the development of the Dene *kede* curriculum and standardizing the Dogrib alphabet in Roman orthography, Lucy became a school principal and is now director of education for the Dogrib Region.

MARGARET PAUL (Passamaquoddy) is a traditional singer and drum keeper with the Wabanoag Singers at St. Mary's Reserve, New Brunswick. In 2002 she was invited to perform for the ambassadors of the world in Paris and in 2003 she sang for Queen Elizabeth on the occasion of her visit to Fredericton. Maggie was also asked to participate on the compact disc *Heartbeat 2: More Voices of First Nations Women,* produced in collaboration with National Museum of American History and Smithsonian Folkways. As a respected elder, Maggie also conducts monthly drumming and singing workshops at Anishnabe Health in Toronto and at the American Indian Health Centre in Detroit.

DAVID W. SAMUELS is associate professor of anthropology at the University of Massachusetts–Amherst. His work on the relationship between music, language, and cultural identity has appeared in *American Ethnologist, Cultural Anthropology,* and *Semiotica.* His book, *Putting a Song on Top of It* (2004), was published by the University of Arizona Press.

LAUREL SERCOMBE is the archivist for the Ethnomusicology Program at the University of Washington in Seattle, a position she has held since 1982. She has coproduced a series of music recordings with Northwest Folklife; lectured for classes in ethnomusicology, library and information science, and American Indian studies; and designed and taught a ten-week course, Introduction to Sound Archiving. She earned a B.A. in music from Humboldt State University, an M.L.S. from the University of Washington, and a Ph.D. in ethnomusicology from the University of Washington in 2001. In 1998 she received a predoctoral Smithsonian Research Fellowship for dissertation research. She is the author of "And Then It Rained: Power and Song in Western Washington Coast Salish Myth Narratives" (dissertation, 2001) and "Ten Early Ethnographers in the Northwest: Recordings from Washington State," in *Spirit of the First People: Native American Music Traditions of Washington State* (University of Washington Press, 1999) and coeditor with William R. Seaburg of *Our Stories: Skagit Myths and Tales* (Lushootseed Press, 2002). Her areas of special interest include Coast Salish literature and songs, the history of ethnographic research in the Pacific Northwest, and the Beatles.

JUDITH VANDER, who lives with her husband in Ojai, California, received her musical training in both composition and ethnomusicology at the University of Michigan. From 1977 to 1997 she researched and wrote about Wind River Shoshone music and culture. In 1989 her book *Songprints: The Musical Experience of Five Shoshone Women* won the ASCAP–Deems Taylor Award as well as the Pauline Alderman Prize for New Scholarship on Women in Music. Another book, *Shoshone Ghost Dance Religion: Poetry Songs and Great Basin Context,* won the Alan Merriam Prize for Outstanding Book in Ethnomusicology in 1998. In addition to these books she has published various articles on Native American culture and music. Since 1998 Vander has returned to composing and has written a song cycle of children's poetry, a string tango for youth orchestra, and a song cycle of William Blake's poetry for adult and children's choirs, piano, and percussion. Using her knowledge of pow-wow music, she has most recently written a three-movement piece titled *Powwow Time* for piano trio.

FRANZISKA VON ROSEN is a documentary filmmaker and adjunct professor of music at Carleton University. She completed her Ph.D. in 1998 with a dissertation on music, "Visual Art and Stories: Conversations with a Community of Micmac Artists." She is a coauthor of *Visions of Sound* (1994) and producer and director of *Celebration of Life* (1995), a social documentary on the healing power of creativity, and *Mi'kmwesu* (2000), an experimental drama exploring a modern urban interpretation of a traditional Mi'kmaq legend and Native drums (in production).

Index

Music in American Life

Louis Prima   *Garry Boulard*

Marian McPartland's Jazz World: All in Good Time   *Marian McPartland*

Robert Johnson: Lost and Found   *Barry Lee Pearson and Bill McCulloch*

Bound for America: Three British Composers   *Nicholas Temperley*

Lost Sounds: Blacks and the Birth of the Recording Industry, 1890–1919
   Tim Brooks

Burn, Baby! BURN! The Autobiography of Magnificent Montague
   Magnificent Montague with Bob Baker

Way Up North in Dixie: A Black Family's Claim to the Confederate
   Anthem   *Howard L. Sacks and Judith Rose Sacks*

The Bluegrass Reader   *Edited by Thomas Goldsmith*

Colin McPhee: Composer in Two Worlds   *Carol J. Oja*

Robert Johnson, Mythmaking, and Contemporary American Culture
   Patricia R. Schroeder

Composing a World: Lou Harrison, Musical Wayfarer   *Leta E. Miller and
   Fredric Lieberman*

Fritz Reiner, Maestro and Martinet   *Kenneth Morgan*

That Toddlin' Town: Chicago's White Dance Bands and Orchestras, 1900–
   1950   *Charles A. Sengstock Jr.*

Dewey and Elvis: The Life and Times of a Rock 'n' Roll Deejay   *Louis Cantor*

Come Hither to Go Yonder: Playing Bluegrass with Bill Monroe   *Bob Black*

Chicago Blues: Portraits and Stories   *David Whiteis*

The Incredible Band of John Philip Sousa   *Paul E. Bierley*

"Maximum Clarity" and Other Writings on Music   *Ben Johnston, edited by
   Bob Gilmore*

Staging Tradition: John Lair and Sarah Gertrude Knott   *Michael Ann Williams*

Homegrown Music: Discovering Bluegrass   *Stephanie P. Ledgin*

Tales of a Theatrical Guru   *Danny Newman*

The Music of Bill Monroe   *Neil V. Rosenberg and Charles K. Wolfe*

Pressing On: The Roni Stoneman Story   *Roni Stoneman, as told to Ellen
   Wright*

Together Let Us Sweetly Live   *Jonathan C. David, with photographs by
   Richard Holloway*

Live Fast, Love Hard: The Faron Young Story   *Diane Diekman*

Air Castle of the South: WSM Radio and the Making of Music City
   Craig P. Havighurst

Traveling Home: Sacred Harp Singing and American Pluralism   *Kiri Miller*

Where Did Our Love Go?: The Rise and Fall of the Motown Sound
   Nelson George

Lonesome Cowgirls and Honky-Tonk Angels: The Women of Barn
   Dance Radio   *Kristine M. McCusker*

California Polyphony: Ethnic Voices, Musical Crossroads   *Mina Yang*

The University of Illinois Press
is a founding member of the
Association of American University Presses.

Composed in 9.5/12.5 Trump Mediaeval
with Myriad display
by Celia Shapland
at the University of Illinois Press
Designed by Dennis Roberts
Manufactured by Sheridan Books, Inc.

University of Illinois Press
1325 South Oak Street
Champaign, IL 61820-6903
www.press.uillinois.edu

Lemon
+
Crow
+
navajo?